A Cookb
Mommy & Me

Learning to be a Little Helper

FAMILY SERIES

Printed in the United States of America
by G&R Publishing Company

Distributed by:
 Products
507 Industrial Street
Waverly, IA 50677

ISBN-13: 978-1-56383-235-2
ISBN-10: 1-56383-235-6

Item #6221

Table of Contents

Drinks

Strawberry Orange Julius

Makes 2 servings

What you'll need

Butter knife
Blender
2 tall glasses

2 straws
Measuring cups and spoons

Ingredients

1 medium banana
½ C. ice
1 scoop ice cream or
   frozen yogurt

½ C. orange juice
1 C. frozen sliced
   strawberries, thawed

Little Helper

With Mommy's help, carefully cut the banana into chunks with the butter knife.

Mommy

Crush the ice in the blender. Measure the remaining ingredients for your Little Helper.

Little Helper

With Mommy's help, put the banana chunks into the blender and add the remaining ingredients. Put the lid on the blender. Push the buttons that Mommy tells you to and blend until well combined.

Mommy

Pour the Orange Julius into the 2 tall glasses.

Little Helper

Add straws and enjoy!

Tootie-Fruitie Smoothie

Makes 2 servings

What you'll need

Butter knife   2 tall glasses

Blender   2 straws

Measuring cups and spoons

Ingredients

1 medium to large banana   1 tsp. vanilla

1 C. orange juice   3 or 4 ice cubes

½ C. milk

─────────── **Little Helper** ───────────

With Mommy's help, carefully cut the banana into chunks with the butter knife. Put banana chunks into the blender.

─────────── **Mommy** ───────────

Measure the orange juice, milk and vanilla for your Little Helper.

─────────── **Little Helper** ───────────

With Mommy's help, pour the orange juice, milk and vanilla into the blender. Add 3 or 4 ice cubes. Place lid on the blender. Push the buttons that Mommy tells you to and blend until well combined.

─────────── **Mommy** ───────────

Pour Tootie-Fruitie Smoothie into the 2 tall glasses.

─────────── **Little Helper** ───────────

Add straws and enjoy!

Brown Cow

Makes 1 serving

What you'll need

Ice cream scoop   Spoon

Glass   Straw

Ingredients

1 scoop vanilla ice cream or   Root beer
  frozen yogurt

───────────── **Little Helper** ─────────────

With Mommy's help, place one scoop of vanilla ice cream into the glass. Pour root beer slowly into glass over the ice cream. Use the spoon or straw to enjoy your Brown Cow!

Cool Cubes

Makes 14 to 16 cubes

What you'll need

Ice cube tray   Straw
Glass

Ingredients

14 to 16 raspberries   Sparkling water or other
Apple juice   clear drink

─────────────── **Little Helper** ───────────────

Place 1 raspberry in each ice cube tray section. With Mommy's help, pour apple juice over the raspberry in each section.

─────────────── **Mommy** ───────────────

Place the ice cube tray in the freezer. When the cubes are solid, carefully remove the cubes from the tray.

─────────────── **Little Helper** ───────────────

Place some of the ice cubes into a clear glass. With Mommy's help, pour sparkling water over the ice cubes. Add straw and enjoy!

Banana Strawberry Smoothie

Makes 2 servings

What you'll need

Butter knife   2 tall glasses
Blender   2 straws
Measuring cups and spoons

Ingredients

1 medium banana   1 scoop ice cream
½ C. crushed ice   or frozen yogurt
½ C. unsweetened apple juice
1 C. chopped strawberries

——————————— Little Helper ———————————

With Mommy's help, carefully cut the banana into chunks with the butter knife. Put banana chunks into the blender.

——————————— Mommy ———————————

Measure the crushed ice, strawberries and apple juice.

——————————— Little Helper ———————————

With Mommy's help, place the crushed ice, strawberries and apple juice into the blender with the banana. Add one scoop of ice cream to the blender. Put the lid on the blender and push the button Mommy tells you to. Blend until smooth.

——————————— Mommy ———————————

Pour the Banana Strawberry Smoothie into the 2 tall glasses.

——————————— Little Helper ———————————

Add straws and enjoy!

Fruity Sparkler

Makes 1 serving

What you'll need

Tall glass
Straw

Spoon

Ingredients

½ C. sliced or chopped fresh
   fruit of your choice
Crushed ice

½ C. any fruit juice
½ C. sparkling water

─────────────── Little Helper ───────────────

With Mommy's help place the fruit and crushed ice in a tall glass.

─────────────── Mommy ───────────────

Add the fruit juice and sparkling water. Mix lightly with the spoon.

─────────────── Little Helper ───────────────

Add a straw and enjoy your Fruity Sparkler!

Dinosaur Punch

Makes 4 to 6 servings

What you'll need

Large pitcher

2 tall glasses

Long handled spoon

2 straws

Ingredients

1 (12 oz. can) frozen lemonade
  concentrate, thawed

1 (12 oz. can) frozen limeade
  concentrate, thawed

1 C. water

1 (1 liter) bottle Sprite

Green food coloring

--------------------- **Mommy** ---------------------

Open the lemonade and limeade concentrates. Measure the water.

--------------------- **Little Helper** ---------------------

With Mommy's help, pour the lemonade and limeade concentrates into a large pitcher. Add the water and Sprite. Stir ingredients together with the long handled spoon while Mommy holds the pitcher.

--------------------- **Mommy** ---------------------

Add the green food coloring while your Little Helper stirs. Place pitcher in the refrigerator to cool. When cool, take out of refrigerator.

--------------------- **Little Helper** ---------------------

Place ice cubes in the 2 tall glasses. With Mommy's help, pour Dinosaur Punch into glasses. Add straws and enjoy!

Caramel Apple Milkshakes

Makes 4 servings

What you'll need

Measuring cups and spoons   4 glasses
Blender   4 straws

Ingredients

3 C. frozen vanilla yogurt   1 tsp. cinnamon
¾ C. milk   ¼ C. caramel topping
½ C. applesauce

Mommy

Measure the yogurt, milk, applesauce, cinnamon and caramel topping.

Little Helper

With Mommy's help, place the yogurt, milk, applesauce, cinnamon and caramel topping into the blender. Place the lid on the blender. Push the button Mommy tells you to.

Mommy

Pour the blended milkshakes into 4 glasses.

Little Helper

Add straws and enjoy!

Chocolate Monkey

Makes 2 servings

What you'll need

Butter knife   2 tall glasses
Blender   2 straws
Measuring cups

Ingredients

1 banana   ½ C. ice cubes
1 C. chocolate milk   1 T. peanut butter

--------------- **Little Helper** ---------------

With Mommy's help, carefully cut the banana into chunks with the butter knife. Put banana chunks into the blender.

--------------- **Mommy** ---------------

Measure the chocolate milk, ice cubes and peanut butter.

--------------- **Little Helper** ---------------

With Mommy's help, place the chocolate milk, ice cubes and peanut butter into the blender with the banana. Push the button Mommy tells you to.

--------------- **Mommy** ---------------

Pour the Chocolate Monkey into the 2 tall glasses.

--------------- **Little Helper** ---------------

Add straws and enjoy!

Breakfast

Monster Toast

Makes 1 serving

What you'll need

Measuring spoons   4 paint brushes
4 glasses   Toaster
Plate   Butter knife

Ingredients

½ C. milk, divided   1 slice bread
Food coloring   Butter

―――――――――― **Mommy** ――――――――――

Pour 2 tablespoons milk in each of the 4 glasses.

―――――――――― **Little Helper** ――――――――――

With Mommy's help, add 1 color of food coloring, a drop at a time, to each glass. This will give you 4 glasses of "paint." Place 1 slice of bread on a plate. With 1 paint brush for each glass, paint the bread however you want. With Mommy's help, place your painted bread in the toaster. Push the toaster knob down to toast the bread.

―――――――――― **Mommy** ――――――――――

Take the slice of toast from the toaster for your Little Helper. Place toasted bread on the plate.

―――――――――― **Little Helper** ――――――――――

With Mommy's help, use the butter knife to lightly butter your toast. Enjoy your painted Monster toast!

The Best Buttermilk Pancakes

Makes nine 6″ pancakes

What you'll need

Electric skillet	Whisk
Measuring cup	Pastry brush
Medium bowl	Spatula

Ingredients

2 C. flour	2 T. sugar
1 tsp. baking powder	2 large eggs, lightly beaten
1 tsp. baking soda	4 C. buttermilk
½ tsp. salt	4 T. butter, melted

─────────────── **Mommy** ───────────────

Heat the electric skillet to 375°. Measure flour, baking powder, baking soda, salt and sugar into a medium bowl.

─────────────── **Little Helper** ───────────────

With Mommy's help, whisk these ingredients together. With Mommy's help, add the eggs.

─────────────── **Mommy** ───────────────

Add buttermilk and 4 tablespoons melted butter. Whisk to combine. Batter should have small to medium lumps. Once skillet is hot, add another ½ teaspoon butter to skillet and spread around evenly.

─────────────── **Little Helper** ───────────────

With Mommy's help, fill the ½ cup measuring cup with pancake batter. Pour onto skillet and make a small pool of batter. Do this again with another ½ cup batter. Pour batter about 2″ away from your last pancake. When pancakes have bubbles on top and are slightly dry around the edges, ask Mommy to flip them over with the spatula so they can cook on the other side for about 1 minute. Keep helping Mommy until all the batter is gone, or eat the pancakes that are done while Mommy finishes cooking the rest.

Cinnamon Almond Oatmeal

Makes 4 servings

What you'll need

Medium saucepan   4 bowls

Measuring cups and spoons   4 spoons

Ingredients

2¼ C. water   1 tsp. cinnamon

¼ tsp. salt   2 T. honey

1½ C. oatmeal   ½ C. chopped almonds

Mommy

In medium saucepan over medium high heat, bring water and salt to a boil. Have your Little Helper watch to tell you when it starts to boil. Add oatmeal and reduce the heat to medium. Stir occasionally, cooking the oats for about 5 minutes.

Little Helper

Remind Mommy to stir the oatmeal every once in a while.

Mommy

Turn off the heat. Add cinnamon and honey and stir until combined. Spoon into 4 bowls.

Little Helper

Sprinkle the chopped almonds on top of oatmeal in bowls. When Mommy says the oatmeal is cool enough, dig in with a spoon and enjoy!

Cheesy Scrambled Eggs

Makes 1 serving

What you'll need

Medium bowl	Spatula
Whisk	Plate
Non-stick pan	Fork

Ingredients

2 eggs	3 T. shredded cheese
Pinch of salt and pepper	

——————— Mommy ———————

Break the eggs into a medium bowl.

——————— Little Helper ———————

With Mommy's help, mix the eggs with a whisk until completely blended. Add salt and pepper.

——————— Mommy ———————

Pour eggs into non-stick pan over medium heat. As the eggs cook, stir with a spatula. When eggs are scrambled, place on the plate.

——————— Little Helper ———————

Sprinkle the shredded cheese over your eggs and mix it up with your fork. When Mommy says the eggs are cool enough, pick up eggs with fork and enjoy!

Crispy French Toast

Makes 3 to 6 servings

What you'll need

Medium bowl	Electric skillet
Measuring cups and spoons	Spatula
2 forks	Plate

Ingredients

2 eggs	¼ tsp. cinnamon
½ C. milk	6 slices bread
¼ tsp. sugar	1 T. oil

─────────── **Mommy** ───────────

Break eggs into medium bowl and beat. Add milk, sugar and cinnamon and mix together.

─────────── **Little Helper** ───────────

Let Mommy help you dip 1 slice of bread into the egg mixture with a fork. Don't let it soak up too much or it will break apart. Just dip the bread in long enough to cover with the egg mixture. Give the bread to Mommy to put on the hot skillet that is covered with the oil. Dip the rest of the bread slices for Mommy as she wants them.

─────────── **Mommy** ───────────

Cook the soaked bread slices on the hot skillet for 2 to 3 minutes. Help your Little Helper to flip them over to cook the other side for another 2 to 3 minutes. When done, remove from skillet and put on the plate.

─────────── **Little Helper** ───────────

Top your French Toast with syrup, powdered sugar, honey or any topping your Mommy gives you. When Mommy says the French toast is ready to eat, pick up your fork and enjoy!

Breakfast Tacos

Makes 4 servings

What you'll need

Skillet	Wire whisk
Paper towels	Spatula
Small bowl	4 plates
Measuring cups	4 forks

Ingredients

4 strips bacon	½ C. shredded Cheddar cheese
4 eggs	Extra sour cream
¼ C. sour cream	Mild salsa
Salt and pepper	
4 flour tortillas	

Mommy

Fry bacon in skillet. Drain on a paper towel, then crumble and set aside. Save bacon drippings.

Little Helper

With Mommy's help, break eggs in a small bowl. Add sour cream and salt and pepper to taste. Mix it all together with a whisk.

Mommy

Pour egg mixture onto the skillet previously used for the bacon and cook for a few minutes. Stir with a spatula and cook eggs until done. Have your Little Helper watch to let you know when the eggs are done.

Little Helper

Place 1 flour tortilla in the middle of a plate. Do this for each tortilla and plate. Have Mommy put the scrambled eggs in the middle of each tortilla. Top the scrambled eggs with the crumbled bacon, shredded cheese, additional sour cream and salsa. With Mommy's help, fold the tortilla shell over the scrambled eggs. Enjoy!

Easy Chocolate Waffles

Makes 4 to 6 servings

What you'll need

Large bowl	Spatula
Medium bowl	4 plates
Waffle iron	4 forks
Non-stick cooking spray	

Ingredients

3 C. flour	⅔ C. sugar
½ T. salt	4 eggs
2 T. baking powder	3½ C. milk
⅔ C. cocoa powder	1 C. vegetable oil

─────── **Mommy** ───────

In large bowl, mix together the flour, salt, baking powder, cocoa powder and sugar and set aside. In medium bowl, break eggs and beat slightly. Stir in the milk and vegetable oil. Add the milk mixture to the dry ingredients and mix together, but make sure you don't overmix. Preheat the waffle iron.

─────── **Little Helper** ───────

Watch Mommy so she doesn't mix the ingredients together too much. Spray the waffle iron with Mommy's help using the non-stick spray.

─────── **Mommy** ───────

Pour approximately 1 cup of the batter at a time onto the waffle iron. Close waffle iron and heat until waffle can be lifted from iron with a spatula or fork. When done, place waffles on the plates.

─────── **Little Helper** ───────

Top your chocolate waffle with syrup, fresh fruit, powdered sugar or any topping your Mommy gives you. Enjoy!

Popeyes

Makes 1 serving

What you'll need

Butter knife   Plate
Frying pan   Fork
Spatula

Ingredients

1 slice of bread   Shredded Cheddar cheese
1 egg

—————————————— Mommy ——————————————
Cut a hole in the middle of the bread slice using the butter knife. Give the center to your Little Helper to eat. Lay bread slice on the greased frying pan over medium heat. Crack an egg and drop into the hole in the center of the bread.

—————————————— Little Helper ——————————————
With Mommy's help, sprinkle the egg and bread slice with shredded Cheddar cheese.

—————————————— Mommy ——————————————
Fry egg and bread until cooked, carefully flipping with the spatula occasionally at even intervals. Scoop out of frying pan and place on the plate.

—————————————— Little Helper ——————————————
Add salt and pepper and enjoy!

Cinnamon Toast

Makes 1 serving

What you'll need

Toaster

Measuring spoons

Butter knife

Toaster oven

Plate

Ingredients

½ tsp. cinnamon

1 tsp. powdered sugar

2 slices bread

2 tsp. butter or margarine

--- **Little Helper** ---

Give 2 slices of bread to Mommy.

--- **Mommy** ---

Place the bread slices into the toaster and toast until golden. While the bread is toasting, measure and mix the cinnamon and sugar together in a small bowl.

--- **Little Helper** ---

With Mommy's help, using the butter knife, spread the toast with butter. Sprinkle the cinnamon and sugar mixture over the buttered toast.

--- **Mommy** ---

Place the toast under broiler or in a toaster oven until glazed, about 1 minute. Place on the plate.

--- **Little Helper** ---

When Mommy says the Cinnamon Toast is ready to eat, pick up and enjoy!

Apple Cinnamon Breakfast Rounds

Makes 2 servings

What you'll need

Sharp knife	2 plates
Measuring cups and spoons	Butter knife
Small bowl	Microwave
Toaster	Spoon

Ingredients

1 red apple	¼ tsp. cinnamon
¼ C. brown sugar	4 English muffins, split
2 T. margarine	½ C. peanut butter

Mommy

Core and slice the apple. Measure the brown sugar, margarine and cinnamon into the small bowl. Split the English muffins and place in toaster. When toasted, place 2 English muffins on each plate.

Little Helper

With Mommy's help, use the butter knife to spread 1 tablespoon peanut butter onto each English muffin half. Top each one with a few apple slices. Place the small bowl with the brown sugar, margarine and cinnamon in the microwave.

Mommy

Show your Little Helper which buttons to push on the microwave to melt the mixture in the small bowl. Take the small bowl out of the microwave and stir until well blended.

Little Helper

With Mommy's help, use the spoon to drizzle the cinnamon mixture over the apple slices. When Mommy says the Apple Cinnamon Breakfast Rounds are ready to eat, pick up and enjoy!

Pretzel Eggs

Makes 2 servings

What you'll need

Small skillet   2 plates
Measuring cups   2 forks
Spatula

Ingredients

1 T. butter   4 eggs
¾ C. mini pretzels

Mommy

Melt the butter in the small skillet over medium high heat. Measure the pretzels.

Little Helper

Give Mommy the 4 eggs so she can crack them into the pan. Give Mommy the pretzels so she can add them to the eggs.

Mommy

Cook, stirring occasionally with spatula, until eggs are set. Divide the eggs onto plates.

Little Helper

When Mommy says the Pretzel Eggs are cool enough to eat, use your fork to dig in and enjoy!

Main Meals

Grilled Cheese Sandwiches

Makes 2 sandwiches

What you'll need

Butter knife   Spatula

Skillet   Plates

Ingredients

4 slices sandwich bread   Cheddar cheese slices

Monterey Jack cheese slices   Butter

─────────────── Little Helper ───────────────

Place 2 slices of bread on the counter or table. Place some of the Monterey Jack cheese slices and some of the Cheddar cheese slices over the bread slices. Top with remaining slices of bread. With Mommy's help, use the butter knife to spread butter onto both outer sides of the sandwiches. Be sure to spread butter all the way to the edges.

─────────────── Mommy ───────────────

Place the sandwiches in a large skillet over medium heat. Press down lightly with the back of the spatula. Cook until golden brown, then flip and cook the other side until the cheese has melted. Heat for about 3 to 4 minutes per side. Place the sandwiches on a plate.

─────────────── Little Helper ───────────────

With Mommy's help, cut the sandwiches in half with the butter knife and enjoy!

Cookie Cutter PB & Jelly

Makes 1 sandwich

What you'll need

Large cookie cutters   Plate
Butter knife

Ingredients

2 slices sandwich bread   Jelly, any kind
Peanut butter

Little Helper

Place 2 slices of bread on the counter or table. Stack one on top of the other. Pick your favorite large cookie cutter. With Mommy's help, press the cookie cutter down through the bread slices. (Eat the outside crust or throw outside for the birds.) With the butter knife, spread peanut butter on top of 1 slice of the cut-out bread. Spread jelly on other slice of cut-out bread. With Mommy's help, put both slices together so your design lines up. Use both hands to pick up and eat.

Mommy

Other items that can be added instead of jelly are raisins, dried cherries, dried apricots or almost anything your Little Helper enjoys!

Fun Taco Cups

Makes 8 to 10 servings

What you'll need

Skillet

Muffin pan

Measuring cups

Spoon

Plate

Fork

Ingredients

1 lb. ground beef

1 pkg. taco seasoning mix

1 (8 oz.) tube
refrigerated biscuits

½ C. shredded
Cheddar cheese

Mommy

Brown the ground beef in the skillet and add the taco seasoning mix. Remove from heat. Preheat oven to 400°.

Little Helper

With Mommy's help, press 1 biscuit into the bottom and up sides of each muffin cup in the muffin pan. With the spoon, scoop the seasoned meat into each muffin cup.

Mommy

Place the Taco Cups in the preheated oven and bake for 15 minutes. Take out of oven and sprinkle the tops of each Taco Cup with shredded Cheddar cheese. Return to oven and bake until the cheese is melted. Take out of oven and carefully transfer 1 or 2 of the Taco Cups onto a plate for your Little Helper.

Little Helper

Top your Taco Cup with your favorite toppings such as diced tomatoes, black olives and lettuce.

Slow Cooker Chicken with Volcano Mashed Potatoes

Makes 6 servings

What you'll need

Slow cooker
Small bowl
Spoons

Plates
Forks

Ingredients

2 (10¾ oz.) cans cream of mushroom soup

1 (10¾ oz.) can cream of chicken soup

1 whole chicken, cut into separate pieces

Instant mashed potato mix

——————————— Mommy ———————————

Place the cream of mushroom and cream of chicken soup in the slow cooker. Stir to mix.

——————————— Little Helper ———————————

With Mommy's help, place the chicken pieces into slow cooker. Wash your hands. Place the lid on the slow cooker and turn the dial to where Mommy tells you to. The chicken will need to cook for 6 to 8 hours on the low setting.

——————————— Mommy ———————————

When the chicken is done cooking, prepare the instant mashed potatoes. Place potatoes in the center of the plate with some of the cooked chicken on the side. Use the sauce from the slow cooker as gravy.

——————————— Little Helper ———————————

Form your potatoes on your plate into a volcano shape. Make a dent with your spoon in the top of your volcano. With Mommy's help, pour some of the gravy over the potatoes to look like it's flowing out of the top of your volcano. Have fun eating!

Corn Dogs

Makes 10 servings

What you'll need

Measuring cups and spoons

Medium bowl

Large skillet

Spatula

Plate

Ingredients

⅔ C. cornmeal

1 egg

⅓ C. flour

2 T. vegetable oil

1 tsp. salt

½ C. milk

10 hot dogs

¼ C. corn oil

Mommy

Combine cornmeal, egg, flour, vegetable oil, salt and milk in medium bowl. Mix well.

Little Helper

With Mommy's help, dip the hot dogs in corn meal mixture turning them to coat all sides.

Mommy

In a large skillet over high heat, place corn oil. When oil is hot, fry the coated hot dogs until golden brown, turning occasionally with the spatula. Once coating is golden, place 1 or 2 corn dogs on a plate for your Little Helper.

Little Helper

When Mommy says the corn dogs are cool enough to eat, enjoy!

Chicken Nuggets

Makes 6 servings

What you'll need

Whisk

Measuring cups and spoons

Small bowl

1 large ziplock bag

Baking sheet

Plate

Fork

Ingredients

1 egg

2 T. milk

3 C. cornflakes, crushed

1 lb. boneless chicken breasts, cut into pieces

Mommy

Preheat oven to 400°. Whisk the egg and milk together in a small bowl and set aside. Place cornflake crumbs in a large ziplock bag. Dip each chicken piece in the egg mixture and place in the bag with the cornflakes. Zip the top of the bag closed. Grease the baking sheet.

Little Helper

Shake the nugget pieces in the cornflake crumb bag until they are all coated. Carefully remove the chicken pieces from the bag and place on the greased baking sheet. Wash your hands.

Mommy

Place the baking sheet in the preheated oven and bake for 15 minutes or until chicken is thoroughly cooked. Carefully remove Chicken Nuggets from oven and place some of them on a plate for your Little Helper.

Little Helper

Use the fork to dip your nuggets into your favorite dipping sauce and enjoy!

Fun & Easy
Pizza Sticks

Makes 6 servings

What you'll need

Baking sheet
Measuring spoons
Small bowl

Plate
Microwave-safe bowl
Microwave

Ingredients

1 (11 oz.) pkg. refrigerated
bread stick dough
12 pepperoni slices
Shredded mozzarella cheese

1 T. grated Parmesan cheese
1 T. Italian seasoning
1 T. garlic powder
Pizza sauce

─────────── Mommy ───────────

Preheat oven to 350°. Open refrigerated bread sticks and separate into six pieces.

─────────── Little Helper ───────────

With Mommy's help, roll the bread sticks out on the ungreased baking sheet. Lay 2 pepperoni slices over each bread stick and sprinkle some shredded mozzarella cheese over each. Fold the bread stick over and twist.

─────────── Mommy ───────────

Mix together the grated Parmesan cheese, Italian seasoning and garlic powder in the small bowl.

─────────── Little Helper ───────────

Use your fingers to sprinkle the Parmesan cheese mixture over top of the twisted bread sticks. Add more mozzarella cheese, if desired.

─────────── Mommy ───────────

Place baking sheet in preheated oven and bake for 5 to 8 minutes or until bread sticks are golden brown. Heat pizza sauce in a microwave-safe bowl in microwave. Place cooked pizza sticks on a plate for your Little Helper.

─────────── Little Helper ───────────

When Mommy says the pizza sticks are ready to eat, dip them into the pizza sauce and enjoy!

Classic
Macaroni & Cheese

Makes 8 to 10 servings

What you'll need

Large pot	Large spoon
Colander	Plate
2-quart casserole dish	Fork
Non-stick cooking spray	

Ingredients

1 (16 oz.) pkg. elbow macaroni	1 T. butter
1 lb. sharp Cheddar cheese, sliced	Salt and pepper to taste
	1 (12 oz.) can evaporated milk

Mommy

Preheat oven to 375°. Bring a large pot filled with lightly salted water to a boil. Add uncooked pasta and cook for 8 to 10 minutes or until al dente. Drain the cooked pasta in the colander. Grease the 2-quart casserole dish with non-stick cooking spray.

Little Helper

With Mommy's help, place ¼ of the cooked macaroni in the bottom of the casserole dish. On top of macaroni layer, place ¼ of the cheese slices in and even layer.

Mommy

Dot some of the butter over the cheese layer. Season with salt and pepper.

Little Helper

With Mommy's help, repeat layering the cooked macaroni and cheese slices three more times. Make sure Mommy tops each layer with some of the butter, salt and pepper.

Mommy

Pour evaporated milk evenly over all the layers. Place in pre-heated oven and bake, uncovered, for 1 hour or until top is golden brown. Remove from oven and let stand for 5 minutes. Spoon Classic Macaroni and Cheese onto plates.

Little Helper

When Mommy says the macaroni and cheese is ready to eat, use your fork to dig in and enjoy!

Ham & Cheddar Roll-Ups

Makes 4 servings

What you'll need

Baking sheet

Butter knife

Measuring cups

Plate

Ingredients

1 (4 oz.) pkg. refrigerated
crescent rolls

Prepared mustard

¼ C. shredded Cheddar cheese

¼ C. finely chopped
cooked ham

─────────── **Mommy** ───────────

Preheat oven to 375°. Unroll crescent rolls and tear along the perforations. Place the 4 crescent dough triangles on the ungreased baking sheet.

─────────── **Little Helper** ───────────

With Mommy's help, use the butter knife to spread mustard lightly over the crescent roll triangles. Sprinkle each triangle with 1 tablespoon shredded cheese and 1 tablespoon chopped ham. Starting at the large end, have Mommy help you roll the dough towards the point. Fold ends in slightly to form a crescent shape.

─────────── **Mommy** ───────────

Place baking sheet in preheated oven and bake for 11 to 13 minutes or until crescent dough is golden brown. Remove Ham & Cheddar Roll-Ups from oven and place 1 or 2 on a plate for your Little Helper.

─────────── **Little Helper** ───────────

When Mommy says the roll-ups are ready to eat, enjoy!

Honey Coated Chicken Fingers

Makes 6 servings

What you'll need

Baking sheet   Plate
Small bowl   Non-stick cooking spray

Ingredients

1 lb. skinless, boneless   ¼ C. water
   chicken breasts   1 C. crushed cornflakes
¼ C. honey

--------------------- **Mommy** ---------------------

Preheat oven to 425°. Spray the baking sheet with non-stick cooking spray. Cut chicken breasts crosswise into ¾″ wide strips. In the small bowl, combine the honey and water. Place crushed cornflakes on a plate.

--------------------- **Little Helper** ---------------------

With Mommy's help, dip the chicken strips in honey mixture. Then place the chicken strips over the crushed cornflakes and turn to coat all sides. Place coated chicken fingers on prepared baking sheet.

--------------------- **Mommy** ---------------------

Place baking sheet in preheated oven and bake for 10 minutes or until chicken fingers are thoroughly cooked, turning chicken over after 5 minutes. Remove chicken fingers from oven and place some on a plate for your Little Helper.

--------------------- **Little Helper** ---------------------

When Mommy says your chicken fingers are ready to eat, pick them up with fingers and enjoy!

Hot Dog Roll-Ups

Makes 8 servings

What you'll need

Baking sheet   Plate
Non-stick cooking spray

Ingredients

1 pkg. hot dogs   1 (8 oz.) can crescent rolls

Mommy

Preheat oven to 400°. Grease the baking sheet with non-stick cooking spray.

Little Helper

With Mommy's help, unroll the crescent rolls one at a time. Roll one crescent roll around each hot dog. Place hot dogs on the greased baking sheet.

Mommy

Place baking sheet in preheated oven and bake for 8 to 10 minutes or until crescent roll dough is light brown. Remove Hot Dog Roll-Ups from oven and place 1 or 2 on a plate for your Little Helper.

Little Helper

When Mommy says the Hot Dog Roll-Ups are ready to eat, dip then in ketchup or mustard and enjoy!

Never-Better Nachos

Makes 2 servings

What you'll need

10 x 15″ jellyroll pan   Plates
Serving platter

Ingredients

16 to 20 tortilla chips   1 T. cooked, crumbled bacon
1¼ C. shredded   or bacon bits
   Cheddar cheese   1 green onion, chopped
2 T. chopped olives   Sour cream or taco sauce

Mommy

Preheat oven to 400°. Spread tortilla chips in a single layer on the jellyroll pan.

Little Helper

With Mommy's help, sprinkle the shredded cheese over the tortilla chips. Sprinkle olives, crumbled bacon and chopped green onion over cheese layer.

Mommy

Place pan in preheated oven and bake for 2 to 3 minutes, or until cheese is melted. Remove pan from oven and transfer nachos to a serving platter. Add dollops of sour cream or taco sauce.

Little Helper

Use your fingers to pick up the nachos and enjoy!

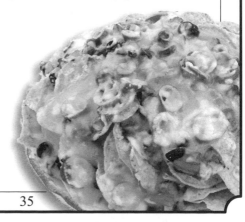

Cheesy Tater Tot Pie

Makes 8 to 10 servings

What you'll need

9 x 13″ baking dish
Measuring cups
Spatula

Aluminum foil
Plate
Fork

Ingredients

1 lb. ground beef
1 C. shredded Cheddar cheese
1 (8 oz.) can French style
   green beans, drained

1 (10¾ oz.) Cheddar
   cheese soup
1 (28 oz.) bag tater tots

Mommy

Preheat oven to 350°. Measure the shredded cheese and open the can of green beans and Cheddar cheese soup.

Little Helper

With Mommy's help, press the ground beef flat into the bottom of the greased baking dish. Spread the cheese soup over the ground beef with the spatula. Spread the drained green beans over top of the cheese. Add the tater tots on top of the green beans. Sprinkle the shredded Cheddar cheese on top.

Mommy

Cover pan with aluminum foil. Place in preheated oven and bake for about 30 minutes or until ground beef is thoroughly cooked. Remove baking dish from oven and take off aluminum foil. Set aside to cool for 5 minutes and pour off any grease from ground beef. Spoon some of the casserole onto a plate for your Little Helper.

Little Helper

When Mommy says the Cheesy Tater Tot Pie is ready to eat, dig in with your fork and enjoy!

Simple Cheesy Muffin Melts

Makes 1 serving

What you'll need

Aluminum foil
Baking sheet

Butter knife
Plate

Ingredients

1 English muffin

2 slices cheese, any kind

——— Mommy ———

Preheat oven to 375°. Cover baking sheet with aluminum foil.

——— Little Helper ———

With Mommy's help, split the English muffin in half with the butter knife. Place English muffin halves on the baking sheet. Top each muffin half with one slice of cheese.

——— Mommy ———

Place baking sheet in preheated oven and bake for about 10 minutes or until cheese is lightly browned and bubbly. Remove from oven and place on a plate for your Little Helper.

——— Little Helper ———

When Mommy says the muffins are ready to eat, enjoy!

Kid's Chef Salad

Makes 6 servings

What you'll need

Salad bowl   Salad tongs

Ingredients

1 head lettuce

⅓ lb. smoked turkey

½ C. shredded Monterey Jack or Swiss cheese

12 red or yellow cherry tomatoes

3 hard-boiled eggs

⅓ C. sliced black olives

Italian dressing

Mommy

Wash, dry and tear the lettuce into bite-sized pieces. Cut the smoked turkey into long, thin strips. Peel and cut the hard-boiled eggs in half.

Little Helper

With Mommy's help, place the lettuce in the salad bowl. Add the turkey strips, shredded cheese, tomatoes, halved eggs and sliced olives over the lettuce.

Mommy

Drizzle the Italian dressing over the salad, toss together lightly with salad tongs and serve.

Robin Hood Wrap

Makes 1 serving

What you'll need

Butter knife

Ingredients

1 tortilla	3 cucumber slices
1 deli ham slice	3 round pickles
1 deli turkey slice	1 T. chopped olives
1 American cheese slice	Mustard
1 Swiss cheese slice	Mayonnaise
¼ C. shredded lettuce	

────── **Little Helper** ──────

Lay the tortilla out flat and use the butter knife to spread a layer of mayonnaise and then a layer of mustard over the tortilla. Layer with the slice of ham and then the slice of turkey. Next, add the slice of American cheese and then the slice of Swiss cheese. Sprinkle the shredded lettuce, olives, cucumbers and pickles over the tortilla. With Mommy's help, roll up the tortilla wrap enclosing all the fillings.

────── **Mommy** ──────

Cut the tortilla wrap into round bite-size pieces. Put on plate for your Little Helper.

Ham & Cheesy Mac

Makes 4 servings

What you'll need

Saucepan
Casserole dish

Plate
Fork

Ingredients

4 C. elbow macaroni
3 T. butter or margarine
½ C. onions, chopped
2 T. flour
Salt to taste
1 can evaporated milk

Salt to taste
1 C. shredded
   American cheese
1 C. shredded Cheddar cheese
1 C. cooked, chopped ham
2 T. bread crumbs

——————— Mommy ———————

Preheat oven to 350°. Cook and drain the elbow macaroni. Set aside.

——————— Little Helper ———————

Place butter in the saucepan.

——————— Mommy ———————

Add chopped onions to the saucepan and sauté in butter for about 3 minutes over medium-high heat. Add flour and salt to taste and stir. Have your Little Helper pour in the evaporated milk. Cook mixture over medium heat until thickened and bubbly. Add cheeses and stir until melted. Remove from heat.

——————— Little Helper ———————

With Mommy's help, stir in the cooked macaroni and chopped ham. Transfer mixture to a casserole dish. Sprinkle top of casserole with bread crumbs.

——————— Mommy ———————

Place casserole dish in preheated oven and bake for 40 minutes. When done, remove from oven and place some Ham & Cheesy Mac on a plate for your Little Helper.

Tortilla Dogs

Makes 1 serving

What you'll need

Microwave-safe plate   Microwave
Toothpick

Ingredients

2 American cheese slices   1 hot dog
1 flour tortilla

Mommy

Cut cheese into ¼" strips.

Little Helper

Place the cheese and the hot dog on the flour tortilla. With Mommy's help, roll it up and stick a toothpick into it to hold it all together. Place the hot dog onto the microwave-safe plate. Place the plate with the hot dog into the microwave. Push the buttons Mommy tells you to on the microwave and cook the wrapped hot dog for 30 seconds to 1 minute. Take out of microwave and, when Mommy says the Tortilla Dog is ready to eat, enjoy!

Easy Cheesy Sketti

Makes 4 servings

What you'll need

Saucepan   Fork
Plate

Ingredients

1 (10¾ oz.) can tomato soup   1¼ C. milk
1 (8 oz.) pkg. processed   ½ lb. spaghetti
   cheese food, cubed, divided

Little Helper

With Mommy's help, combine the tomato soup and milk in the saucepan. Add half of the cubed cheese.

Mommy

Cook and drain the spaghetti. Place the saucepan over medium heat until melted, stirring constantly. Continue to add the cheese, melting all together, but be careful not to boil. Add more milk until desired consistency is reached. Remove from heat. Place warm, cooked spaghetti on plate and cover with the sauce mixture for your Little Helper.

Mini Pizzas

Makes 4 to 8 servings

What you'll need

Butter knife   Baking sheet
Toaster   Plate

Ingredients

4 English muffins   Assorted pizza toppings
1 (8 oz.) can pizza sauce
1 C. shredded
   mozzarella cheese

─────────────── **Little Helper** ───────────────

With Mommy's help, split the English muffins with the butter knife. Put the English muffin halves into the toaster and push the button down to start the toaster.

─────────────── **Mommy** ───────────────

Preheat oven to 400°. Remove the English muffins from the toaster when lightly toasted and place them on the baking sheet.

─────────────── **Little Helper** ───────────────

With Mommy's help, spread 1 tablespoon of pizza sauce over each muffin half with the butter knife. Sprinkle each half with some of the shredded cheese. Then top with your favorite pizza topping, such as green peppers, mushrooms or pepperoni.

─────────────── **Mommy** ───────────────

Place the baking sheet in the preheated oven and bake for about 6 minutes, or until the cheese melts. Remove from oven and place 1 or 2 of the pizzas on the plate for your Little Helper.

Awesome Broccoli & Cheese Bake

Makes 8 servings

What you'll need

9 x 13″ baking dish
Measuring cups
Medium bowl
Whisk

Large bowl
Fork
Rubber spatula
Plate

Ingredients

1 (10¾ oz.) can cream of
  mushroom soup
1 C. mayonnaise
1 egg, beaten
¼ C. onion, chopped
3 (10 oz.) pkgs. frozen
  chopped broccoli

1 C. shredded sharp
  Cheddar cheese
Salt and pepper to taste
Pinch of paprika

Mommy

Preheat oven to 350°. Grease the baking dish. Chop and measure the ingredients for your Little Helper.

Little Helper

With Mommy's help, in the medium mixing bowl, whisk together the cream of mushroom soup, mayonnaise, egg and chopped onion. Place the broccoli into the large mixing bowl. With Mommy's help, break up the frozen broccoli with the fork.

Mommy

Using the rubber spatula, spread the soup mixture on top of the broccoli and mix well. Sprinkle with cheese and mix well. Spread the mixture into the prepared baking dish. Smooth the top of the casserole with the rubber spatula. Season with salt, pepper and paprika. Place in the preheated oven for 45 minutes to 1 hour. Remove from oven and place some of the Awesome Broccoli and Cheese Bake onto the plate for your Little Helper.

Crispy Bacon Tortilla

Makes 1 serving

What you'll need

Microwave-safe plate   Plate

Paper towels   Microwave

Ingredients

1 tortilla   2 slices American cheese

2 pieces bacon

Little Helper

Place 2 pieces of bacon on the microwave-safe plate and cover with a paper towel. Place the plate in the microwave. Push the buttons Mommy tells you to in order to cook the bacon for 2 minutes.

Mommy

Take the cooked bacon out of microwave when done and drain bacon on dry paper towels.

Little Helper

Place the tortilla on the plate and add the cheese slices. Put the plate back into the microwave and push the buttons Mommy tells you to, heating the tortilla and cheese for about 20 seconds.

Mommy

Take the tortilla out of microwave when the cheese is melted.

Little Helper

Put the cooked bacon over the cheese and, with Mommy's help, roll up your tortilla. Add toppings of your choice and enjoy!

Layers & Layers of Dinner

Makes 6 servings

What you'll need

1½ quart baking dish
Small bowl
Measuring cups and spoons

Small glass bowl
Plate
Fork

Ingredients

1 (16 oz.) can cut green
   beans, drained
8 slices cooked ham
1 (10½ oz.) can cream of
   celery soup

¼ C. mayonnaise
1 tsp. prepared mustard
5 slices American cheese
1 T. margarine
⅓ C. seasoned croutons

——— Little Helper ———

With Mommy's help, pour the drained green beans into the 1½ quart glass baking dish. Top with the slices of cooked ham. In a small bowl, combine the cream of celery soup, mayonnaise and mustard. Blend well. Pour the soup mixture over the meat slices. Top with the 5 slices of cheese.

——— Mommy ———

Place margarine in a small glass bowl and melt in microwave for 15 seconds. Toss the croutons in the melted butter.

——— Little Helper ———

Sprinkle the buttered croutons over the cheese.

——— Mommy ———

Place the uncovered baking dish in the microwave oven and show your Little Helper which buttons to push. Microwave for 10 minutes. Take casserole from the microwave. Let stand for 5 minutes before serving. Scoop some of the casserole onto the plate for your Little Helper.

Impossible
Burrito Bake

Makes 4 servings

What you'll need

Measuring cups and spoons   Medium skillet
Medium bowl   Plate
Pie plate   Fork

Ingredients

1 C. biscuit baking mix   Salt and pepper to taste
⅓ C. water   1 C. salsa
1 (16 oz.) can refried beans   1 C. shredded Cheddar
1 lb. ground beef   cheese

--- **Mommy** ---

Preheat oven to 350°. Mix the biscuit baking mix, water and refried beans together in the medium bowl.

--- **Little Helper** ---

Help Mommy transfer the mixture into the bottom of the greased pie plate.

--- **Mommy** ---

Brown and drain the ground beef in the skillet. Season with salt and pepper.

--- **Little Helper** ---

Scoop the seasoned ground beef over the mixture in the pie plate. Top with the salsa and shredded Cheddar cheese.

--- **Mommy** ---

Place the uncovered pie plate in the preheated oven and bake for 30 minutes or until golden brown. Remove pie plate from the oven and let sit for about 15 minutes. Cut into sections like a pie. Place a slice onto the plate for your Little Helper.

Kid Friendly Meat Loaf

Makes 8 servings

What you'll need

Large bowl   Plate
Measuring cups   Fork
9 x 13″ baking dish

Ingredients

1 env. dry onion soup mix   2 eggs
2 lbs. ground beef   ¾ C. water
1½ C. bread crumbs   ⅓ C. ketchup

——————————— Mommy ———————————

Preheat oven to 350°.

——————————— Little Helper ———————————

With Mommy's help, combine dry onion soup mix, ground beef, bread crumbs, eggs, water and ketchup in the large bowl. Mix it all together with your cleaned hands. Wash hands.

——————————— Mommy ———————————

Shape the ground beef mixture into a loaf and place in the 9 x 13″ baking dish. Place the baking dish in the preheated oven and bake for 1 hour or until done. Remove from oven and let set for 5 minutes. Cut into slices and place a slice onto the plate for your Little Helper.

——————————— Little Helper ———————————

When Mommy says the meat loaf is ready to eat, use your fork to dip the bites in ketchup or mustard and enjoy!

Goldfish Tuna Casserole

Makes 8 servings

What you'll need

Cooking pot   Plate
Large casserole dish   Fork

Ingredients

2 pkgs. flat noodles
2 (6 oz.) cans tuna in water,
  drained
2 (10¾ oz.) cans cream
  of mushroom soup

2 C. milk
2 tsp. seasoning salt
1 (6½ oz.) pkg. Goldfish
  Cheddar crackers

Mommy

Preheat oven to 350°. Cook the noodles in the large cooking pot.

Little Helper

While the noodles are cooking, with Mommy's help, combine the drained tuna, cream of mushroom soup, milk and seasoning salt in the large casserole dish.

Mommy

Drain the noodles and add to the mixture in the casserole dish.

Little Helper

Sprinkle the Goldfish Cheddar crackers over the casserole mixture.

Mommy

Place the casserole dish in the preheated oven and bake for 10 to 15 minutes. Remove from the oven and place some of the Goldfish Tuna Casserole onto a plate for your Little Helper.

Potato Ham Casserole

Makes 7 servings

What you'll need

Slow cooker	Plate
Measuring cups and spoons	Fork
Small bowl	

Ingredients

6 C. potatoes, peeled and sliced	1 can cream of mushroom soup
1 medium onion, coarsely chopped	½ C. milk
1½ C. ham, cooked and cubed	¼ tsp. dried thyme
1 C. shredded American cheese	

Mommy

Prepare the vegetables and measure the ingredients for your Little Helper.

Little Helper

With Mommy's help, layer half of the potatoes, half of the onion, half of the ham and half of the cheese in the bottom of the slow cooker. Repeat layers with the remaining ingredients.

Mommy

In the small bowl, combine the cream of mushroom soup, milk and dried thyme. Pour mixture over the layers in the slow cooker. Place lid on the slow cooker.

Little Helper

With Mommy's help, turn the dial on the slow cooker to the high setting. After 1 hour of cooking on high, turn the dial to the low setting and let the casserole cook for 6 to 8 hours or until the potatoes are tender.

Mommy

Take the cover off the slow cooker and place some of the Potato Ham Casserole on the plate for your Little Helper.

Fresh Veggie Pizza

Makes 4 servings

What you'll need

Pizza pan   Spatula
Measuring cups   Plate
Medium bowl

Ingredients

1 (10″ or 12″) prepared   1 C. sour cream
  pizza crust   1 env. Ranch dressing mix
1 (8 oz.) pkg. cream cheese,   2 C. raw vegetables,
  softened   finely chopped

—— Mommy ——

Preheat oven to 350°. Place the prepared pizza crust onto the pizza pan. Bake in preheated oven without toppings for 5 to 10 minutes, until light brown.

—— Little Helper ——

With Mommy's help, stir together the cream cheese, sour cream and dressing mix together in the medium bowl. With the spatula, spread the cream cheese mixture over the pizza crust. Top with your favorite vegetables, such as broccoli, cauliflower, carrots, cucumbers and tomatoes.

—— Little Helper ——

Cut the Fresh Veggie Pizza into slices and place a slice on the plate for your Little Helper.

Pennies & Potatoes

Makes 6 servings

What you'll need

1 quart casserole dish

Non-stick cooking spray

Measuring cups and spoons

Small bowl

Long handled spoon

Plate

Fork

Ingredients

4 C. potatoes, cooked
   and diced

1 onion, chopped

1 pkg. hot dogs, sliced

3 T. margarine

3 T. flour

1¼ C. milk

1½ C. shredded Cheddar
   or American cheese

Mommy

Preheat oven to 450°. Grease the 1 quart casserole dish with the non-stick cooking spray. Prepare and measure the ingredients for your Little Helper.

Little Helper

With Mommy's help, place the diced potatoes, chopped onions and sliced hot dogs in the casserole dish.

Mommy

Heat the margarine in the small bowl in the microwave for 15 seconds. Mix in the flour and milk and heat for 30 seconds, stirring occasionally, until it becomes a little thick. Stir in the shredded cheese.

Little Helper

With Mommy's help, pour the cheese mixture over the ingredients in the casserole dish. Sprinkle some more shredded cheese on top.

Mommy

Place the casserole dish in the preheated oven and bake for 30 minutes. Remove from oven and place some of the Pennies & Potatoes on the plate for your Little Helper.

Bean Burgers

Makes 4 servings

What you'll need

Large bowl	Spoon
Measuring cups	Plate
Baking sheet	Fork

Ingredients

1 lb. ground beef, browned and drained	½ medium onion, chopped
2 (11 oz.) cans pork and beans	4 hamburger buns
	½ C. grated Parmesan cheese

_____ Mommy _____

Preheat oven to 450°. Mix together ground beef, beans and chopped onion in the large bowl.

_____ Little Helper _____

With Mommy's help, separate the buns and place them, open faced, on a baking sheet. Spoon the meat mixture over the buns. Sprinkle grated Parmesan cheese on top of the meat mixture.

_____ Mommy _____

Place the cookie sheet into the preheated oven and bake for 8 to 10 minutes. Remove from the oven just as the cheese is beginning to brown. Place a Bean Burger onto the plate for your Little Helper.

Chicken & Rice

Makes 4 servings

What you'll need

9 x 13″ baking dish
Bowl
Measuring cups

Aluminum foil
Plate
Fork

Ingredients

2 C. long grain white rice, uncooked

4 chicken breast halves

Salt and pepper to taste

1 (10¾ oz.) can cream of celery soup

1 (10¾ oz.) can cream of mushroom soup

1 (1 oz.) pkg. onion soup mix

2½ C. chicken broth

Little Helper

With Mommy's help, spread the uncooked rice evenly across the bottom of the greased 9 x 13″ baking dish. Place the chicken breast halves on top of the rice.

Mommy

Sprinkle the chicken breast halves with salt and pepper. Preheat the oven to 350°. Mix the cream of celery soup and cream of mushroom soup together in the bowl. Spread the soup mixture over the chicken breasts.

Little Helper

With Mommy's help, sprinkle the dry onion soup mix on top. Pour the chicken broth over the entire casserole.

Mommy

Cover the baking dish with aluminum foil. Place the casserole into the preheated oven and bake for 1½ hours. Remove from oven and let cool slightly. Place a serving onto the plate for your Little Helper.

Tomato Soup

Makes 8 servings

What you'll need

Saucepan   Bowl
Measuring cups and spoons   Spoon

Ingredients

1 (28 oz.) can diced tomatoes   2 T. sugar
   in juice   1 T. chopped onion
1 C. chicken broth   ⅛ tsp. baking soda
¼ C. butter   2 C. milk

──────────── **Little Helper** ────────────

With Mommy's help, combine the diced tomatoes in juice, chicken broth, butter, sugar, chopped onion and baking soda in the saucepan. Mix lightly.

──────────── **Mommy** ────────────

Place the cover on the saucepan and set over medium heat to simmer for 1 hour, stirring occasionally.

──────────── **Little Helper** ────────────

With Mommy's help, heat milk in microwave just until warm. Stir the warm milk into the tomato mixture in the saucepan just before serving.

──────────── **Mommy** ────────────

Ladle some Tomato Soup into the bowl for your Little Helper.

Basic Meatballs

Makes 6 servings

What you'll need

Large bowl

Whisk

Measuring cups and spoons

Large skillet

Slotted spoon

Paper towels

Plate

Fork

Ingredients

1 large egg

1 lb. ground beef

⅓ C. dry bread crumbs

¼ C. chopped onion

¼ C. milk

1 tsp. Worcestershire sauce

¾ tsp. salt

⅛ tsp. pepper

2 T. vegetable oil

Little Helper

With Mommy's help, whisk the egg in the large bowl.

Mommy

Add the ground beef, bread crumbs, chopped onion, milk, Worcestershire sauce, salt and pepper.

Little Helper

With clean hands, mix it all together until combined. With Mommy's help, gently shape the mixture into meatballs. Wash your hands.

Mommy

Heat the vegetable oil in the large skillet over medium high heat. When hot, but not smoking, add meatballs and heat until browned and thoroughly cooked, about 15 to 18 minutes. Remove meatballs with a slotted spoon and drain on paper towels. Place some Basic Meatballs on the plate for your Little Helper or stir into a spaghetti sauce or other recipe calling for meatballs.

Treats,
Cookies &
Desserts

Angel Cookies For Easy Bake Oven

Makes 12 servings

What you'll need

Measuring spoons

Small bowl

Spoon

Baking sheet

Easy Bake Oven

Ingredients

6 tsp. butter

3 tsp. sugar

3 tsp. brown sugar

Pinch of salt

¼ C. flour

⅛ tsp. cream of tartar

⅛ tsp. baking soda

—————————— Little Helper ——————————

With Mommy's help, measure and cream together the butter, sugars and salt in a small bowl. Add flour, cream of tartar and baking soda. Mix until well combined. Place 12 spoonfuls of the dough onto the baking sheet. Bake for 5 minutes in an Easy Bake Oven. Ask Mommy to help you remove the baking sheet from the oven. Make sure to use a hot pad because the pan may be hot!

Banana Blasters

Makes 1 serving

What you'll need

Butter knife   Paper plate
1 popsicle stick

Ingredients

1 banana   Wheat germ
Honey   Granola

——————————— **Little Helper** ———————————

With Mommy's help, peel the banana. With the butter knife, cut the banana in half crosswise so you have two equal parts. Push a popsicle stick in the flat end. Pour honey onto the paper plate. Roll the banana, using the popsicle stick, in the honey until it is fully coated. Sprinkle the coated banana with wheat germ or granola. Eat and enjoy!

Bacon & Eggs Candy

What you'll need

Double boiler   **Spoon**
Waxed paper

Ingredients

Small pretzel sticks   **Yellow M&M's**
White chocolate or coating

Mommy

In a double boiler over simmering water, heat white chocolate until melted.

Little Helper

With Mommy's help, lay 3 pretzel sticks side by side on waxed paper. Place a small dollop of melted white chocolate in the center to hold the pretzels together and form the "egg white". Place one yellow M&M in center of chocolate for the "yolk". Repeat with remaining pretzels, chocolate and M&M's. Let the chocolate harden at room temperature. Peel off the waxed paper when Mommy says the Bacon & Eggs Candies are ready and enjoy!

Rice Cake S'mores

Makes 1 serving

What you'll need

Butter knife   Microwave
Microwave-safe plate

Ingredients

Peanut butter   ½ (1 oz.) bar milk chocolate
Plain rice cake   Tiny marshmallows

—————————— **Little Helper** ——————————

With Mommy's help, spread the peanut butter over the rice cake. Place on a microwave-safe plate. Top the rice cake with the chocolate piece and a few marshmallows. Do not cover. Place the plate in the microwave. Push the buttons Mommy tells you to in order to cook on high for 18 to 20 seconds. Take out of microwave and wait for about 1 minute before eating. Enjoy!

Cinnamon Snails

Makes 4 servings

What you'll need

Non-stick cooking spray   Waxed paper
Baking sheet   Rolling pin
Measuring cups and spoons   Plate
Small bowl

Ingredients

3 T. sugar   1 (8 oz.) pkg. refrigerated
¼ C. chopped nuts   breadsticks
½ tsp. cinnamon

Mommy

Preheat oven to 375°. Lightly coat the baking sheet with non-stick cooking spray.

Little Helper

With Mommy's help, combine the sugar, cinnamon and nuts in the small bowl. Sprinkle this mixture over the waxed paper placed on top of the counter. Unroll 1 breadstick. Tightly roll into a coil. Unwrap another breadstick and roll around the coil, forming a larger coil. Place the large coil onto the sugared surface on the waxed paper. Roll with rolling pin to ⅛″ thickness. Place on the baking sheet with the sugared side up. Repeat with the remaining 6 breadsticks.

Mommy

Place the baking sheet in the preheated oven and bake for about 15 minutes or until golden. Remove from oven and place a Cinnamon Snail on the plate for your Little Helper.

Fun Rainbow Cookie Pops

Makes 10 servings

What you'll need

10 popsicle sticks	Waxed paper
Microwave-safe bowl	Baking sheet
Paper plates	

Ingredients

20 vanilla wafer cookies	Colored sprinkles
½ C. peanut butter	M&M's candies
1 (6 oz.) bag white chocolate chips	M&M's mini candies

Little Helper

With Mommy's help, spread the peanut butter on the flat side of each vanilla wafer cookie. Place a popsicle stick into the peanut butter on half the cookies. Top with another cookie so the stick is between the 2 cookies, forming 10 cookie pops.

Mommy

Melt the white chocolate chips in the microwave-safe bowl in the microwave for 1 minute, then in 20 second increments, stirring until smooth.

Little Helper

With Mommy's help, place the sprinkles, M&M's candies and M&M's mini candies on separate paper plates. Dip the cookie pops in the melted white chocolate, covering completely. Roll the pops in the sprinkles, M&M's candies or M&M's mini candies and place them on the baking sheet covered with waxed paper.

Mommy

Place the baking sheet in refrigerator to chill and harden the white chocolate. When ready, remove from refrigerator and give one to your Little Helper.

Frozen Bananas

Makes 1 serving

What you'll need

Butter knife   Plastic bag
Skewers   Small bowls
Baking sheet

Ingredients

Bananas   Applesauce
Yogurt   Wheat germ
Peanut butter   Finely chopped nuts
Melted chocolate   Shredded coconut

——————————————— Little Helper ———————————————

With Mommy's help, cut the bananas in half crosswise with the butter knife. Insert the skewers in the flat end. Place the bananas on a baking sheet.

——————————————— Mommy ———————————————

Place the baking sheet with the bananas in the freezer. When frozen, place frozen banana skewers in a plastic bag. Keep frozen until ready to use. Take banana out a little before needed to allow to thaw slightly before eating.

——————————————— Little Helper ———————————————

Eat the banana plain, or with Mommy's help, place your favorite toppings in small bowls. Before each bite, dip banana into either the yogurt, peanut butter, melted chocolate or applesauce and then into either the wheat germ, chopped nuts or shredded coconut. See what kind of delicious combinations you can make and enjoy!

Easy Chocolate Cookie Spots for Kids

Makes about 24

What you'll need

Baking sheets   Plate

Ingredients

1 (12 oz.) box vanilla   M&M's candies
  wafer cookies   Candy hearts
1 (13 oz.) bag Hershey's Kisses

—————————— **Mommy** ——————————

Preheat oven to 200°.

—————————— **Little Helper** ——————————

With Mommy's help, place the vanilla wafer cookies 1″ apart on the ungreased baking sheet. Place one Hershey's Kiss on the center of each cookie.

—————————— **Mommy** ——————————

Place baking sheet in preheated oven for 5 minutes. Remove from oven and gently press an M&M candy or a candy heart into the center of the softened Hershey's Kiss. Let set until the chocolate hardens again. Place 1 or 2 Chocolate Cookie Spots on the plate for your Little Helper to enjoy!

Chocolate Cornflake Surprises

Makes 12 servings

What you'll need

Double boiler   Muffin pan
Measuring cups   Plate
Spoon

Ingredients

5 miniature Mars candy bars   6 C. cornflakes

─────────────── Mommy ───────────────

Place the Mars bars in a double boiler, or in a bowl over boiling water, and stir until melted.

─────────────── Little Helper ───────────────

With Mommy's help, add the cornflakes to the melted candy bars. Mix quickly since the chocolate hardens very quickly. Add more cornflakes if needed. Divide the cornflakes mixture into 12 greased muffin cups.

─────────────── Mommy ───────────────

Place the muffin pan in the refrigerator until the chocolate has hardened. Remove from refrigerator and place a Chocolate Cornflake Surprise on the plate for your Little Helper to enjoy!

Bugs & Dirt

Makes 4 servings

What you'll need

Large plastic bag
Rolling pin
Large bowl

Sand shovel
Small bowl
Spoon

Ingredients

6 chocolate graham crackers
1 T. chocolate sprinkles (ants)
1 T. raisins (beetles)

8 gummy worms
1 C. prepared
   chocolate pudding

—————————————— **Little Helper** ——————————————

With Mommy's help, put the chocolate graham crackers into a plastic bag and seal the bag, making sure there is no air in the bag. Crush the graham crackers with a rolling pin. Pour the crushed graham crackers into a large bowl, then add the ants, beetles and worms to the "dirt." Add the chocolate pudding and stir it all together. Use the sand shovel to scoop up some "dirt and bugs" and place in the small bowl. Use your spoon to dig up some Bugs & Dirt and enjoy!

Homemade Mints

Makes about 20

What you'll need

Measuring cups and spoons
Large bowl
Wooden spoon

2 paper plates
Fork
Plastic wrap

Ingredients

⅓ C. butter, softened
⅓ C. light corn syrup
½ tsp. salt

½ C. powdered sugar, sifted
1 tsp. flavoring
Food coloring

——————————— **Mommy** ———————————

Measure the butter, corn syrup, salt and powdered sugar into the large bowl.

——————————— **Little Helper** ———————————

With Mommy's help, stir the mixture with the wooden spoon until it becomes too stiff to stir. Then knead the mixture with clean hands on a flat surface sprinkled with powdered sugar until the dough is smooth. Add your favorite flavoring and/or food coloring.

——————————— **Mommy** ———————————

Place a portion of the dough on the paper plate for your Little Helper.

——————————— **Little Helper** ———————————

Pinch off small pieces of dough and roll them into balls. Press the balls lightly with a fork to make a fancy mint or press into a mint mold. Place your mints on a separate paper plate.

——————————— **Mommy** ———————————

Place the plate of mints in the refrigerator for 30 minutes or until they are firm. Cover them with plastic wrap to keep your Little Helper from eating them all.

——————————— **Little Helper** ———————————

Try not to eat too many today, because the mints always taste better on the second day.

Chocolate Spiders

Makes about 15

What you'll need

Microwave-safe bowl
Microwave
Baking sheet

Waxed paper
Spoon
Plate

Ingredients

1 (12 oz.) pkg.
chocolate chips
1 (12 oz.) pkg.
butterscotch chips

1 (5 oz.) can chow
mein noodles
1½ C. peanuts

─────────── **Mommy** ───────────

Place the chocolate and butterscotch chips into the bowl and heat in the microwave for 20 seconds. Stir chocolate and butterscotch chips. Return to microwave for another 20 seconds and stir. Continue heating and stirring until mixture is completely melted.

─────────── **Little Helper** ───────────

With Mommy's help, stir the chow mein noodles and peanuts into the melted chips and mix well. Scoop some of the mixture with the spoon and drop onto the baking sheet that has been covered with waxed paper. Continue until baking sheet is covered.

─────────── **Mommy** ───────────

Place the baking sheet in the refrigerator to set. After about 10 minutes, remove baking sheet from refrigerator and place 1 or 2 Spiders on the plate for your Little Helper.

Reindeer Food

Makes about 10 cups

What you'll need

Double boiler   Wooden spoon
Measuring spoons   Waxed paper
Large bowl

Ingredients

16 oz. white chocolate   3 C. pretzels
3 C. Crispix   1 (12 oz.) pkg. miniature
3 C. Cheerios   M&M's baking bits

─────────── Mommy ───────────

Place the white chocolate in a double boiler over simmering water. Heat, stirring often, until chocolate is completely melted. Help your Little Helper measure the Crispix, Cheerios and pretzels into the large bowl.

─────────── Little Helper ───────────

With Mommy's help, pour the melted white chocolate over the cereal and pretzels in the large bowl. Mix with wooden spoon. Add the M&M's after the chocolate has cooled slightly so they won't melt when mixed in.

─────────── Mommy ───────────

Pour mixture onto the waxed paper.

─────────── Little Helper ───────────

Spread the mixture over the waxed paper with the wooden spoon. When Mommy says the chocolate has cooled and hardened, break the Reindeer Food into pieces and enjoy!

Popcorn Balls

Makes about 12

What you'll need

Large saucepan   Waxed paper
Wooden spoon   Large bowl

Ingredients

10 to 12 C. popped popcorn   ¾ C. butter
1 (1 lb.) bag marshmallows

Mommy

Place the popped popcorn in a very large bowl.

Little Helper

With Mommy's help, place the butter in the large saucepan.

Mommy

Melt the butter over low heat and add the marshmallows. Cook until marshmallows are gooey. Pour the melted marshmallows over the bowl of popcorn and mix until the popcorn is coated.

Little Helper

When Mommy says the mixture is cool enough, moisten your hands with cold water and form into balls. Place the balls on the waxed paper. When Mommy says the Popcorn Balls are ready to eat, enjoy one!

Ice Cream Sandwich Dessert

Makes 12 to 15 servings

What you'll need

Butter knife

9 x 13″ baking dish

Measuring cup

Spoon

Aluminum foil

Ingredients

19 ice cream sandwiches

1 (12 oz.) tub frozen whipped topping, thawed

1 (11¾ oz.) jar hot fudge topping

1 C. salted peanuts

Mommy

Cut one ice cream sandwich in half with the butter knife. Place one whole and one half sandwich along the short side of the pan. Arrange 8 sandwiches in opposite direction in the 9 x 13″ baking dish.

Little Helper

With Mommy's help, spread half of the whipped topping over the ice cream sandwiches. Spoon the fudge topping over the whipped topping. Sprinkle half of the peanuts over the fudge topping.

Mommy

Place another layer of ice cream sandwiches over the peanut layer, using the remaining 9½ ice cream sandwiches.

Little Helper

With Mommy's help, spread another layer of whipped topping and peanuts over the ice cream sandwiches. The pan will be full.

Mommy

Cover the pan with aluminum foil and place in freezer until frozen. May freeze for up to 2 weeks. Remove from the freezer 20 minutes before serving. Cut into squares to serve.

Shake & Make
Ice Cream

Makes 1 serving

What you'll need

Measuring cups and spoons   Bowl
Large ziplock bag   Spoon
Small ziplock bag

Ingredients

Ice cubes   1 C. half n' half
1 T. rock salt   ½ tsp. vanilla
2 T. sugar

Little Helper

With Mommy's help, fill the large ziplock bag half full of ice cubes.

Mommy

Add the rock salt to the bag of ice and seal. Pour the sugar, half n' half and vanilla into the small ziplock bag and seal.

Little Helper

With Mommy's help, place the small ziplock bag inside the large bag and seal. Take turns shaking the bag with Mommy for 5 to 7 minutes.

Mommy

Remove the small bag from the large bag. Open the small bag and spoon the ice cream into the bowl for your Little Helper. Discard the large bag with ice and salt.

No Bake
Crispy Squares

Makes 8 to 10 servings

What you'll need

Large bowl
Measuring cups and spoons
Medium saucepan

9 x 13″ baking dish
Butter knife
Plate

Ingredients

4 C. Cheerios
2 C. crispy rice cereal
2 C. dry roasted peanuts
2 C. M&M's

1 C. light corn syrup
1 C. sugar
1½ C. creamy peanut butter
1 tsp. vanilla

—————— Little Helper ——————

With Mommy's help, measure the Cheerios, crispy rice cereal, dry roasted peanuts and M&M's into the large bowl. Set aside.

—————— Mommy ——————

In the medium saucepan over medium heat, bring the corn syrup and sugar to a boil, stirring frequently. Remove from heat and stir in the peanut butter and vanilla. Pour over the cereal mixture and toss until evenly coated. Spread into the greased 9 x 13″ baking dish, spread evenly and let cool. When cool, cut the No Bake Crispy Squares with the butter knife and place on the plate for your Little Helper.

Pumpkin Pie

Makes 6 to 8 servings

What you'll need

Baking sheet	Rubber spatula
9″ pie pan	Butter knife
Large bowl	Plate
Measuring cups and spoons	Fork

Ingredients

1 (9″) prepared pie crust	1 tsp. cinnamon
2 large eggs	½ tsp. ground ginger
1 (15 oz.) can pumpkin	¼ tsp. ground cloves
¼ C. sugar	1 (12 oz.) can evaporated milk
½ tsp. salt	

——— Little Helper ———

With Mommy's help, place the baking sheet on a rack near the bottom of the oven. Help Mommy place the prepared pie crust in a 9″ pie pan.

——— Mommy ———

Preheat oven to 425°. Break the eggs into the large bowl and beat slightly. With your Little Helper, measure the pumpkin, sugar, salt, cinnamon, ground ginger, ground cloves and evaporated milk into the bowl and mix well. Pour the filling into the pie crust in pie pan. Reduce the oven temperature to 350°. Place pie in oven and bake for 40 to 50 minutes, or until a butter knife inserted near the center comes out clean. Remove from oven and place on a wire rack. Cool completely. When cooled, cover and place in refrigerator to chill. When the pie is chilled, remove from the refrigerator.

——— Little Helper ———

With Mommy's help, cut the pie into individual pieces. Have Mommy put 1 slice on your plate and enjoy.

Marshmallow Snowflakes

Makes 100 marshmallows

What you'll need

Jellyroll pans	Medium saucepan
Candy thermometer	Parchment paper
Electric mixer	Spatula

Ingredients

Non-stick cooking spray	⅔ C. light corn syrup
⅔ C. cold water, divided	⅛ tsp. salt
2 envs. unflavored gelatin	1 tsp. vanilla
1½ C. sugar	

Little Helper

With Mommy's help, spray two jellyroll pans with the non-stick cooking spray and line with the parchment paper. Grease the parchment paper and set pan aside. Pour ⅓ cup cold water into bowl of the electric mixer. Sprinkle with the gelatin. Let mixture soften, about 5 minutes.

Mommy

Place the sugar, corn syrup, salt and water mixture in the medium saucepan. Over medium heat, cover and bring to a boil. Remove the lid. Heat, swirling pan occasionally, until the syrup reaches 238° (soft ball stage) on a candy thermometer, about 5 minutes. Beat the gelatin mixture at low speed and carefully pour the syrup in a steady steam down the side of the bowl to avoid splattering. Gradually increase the speed to high and beat until mixture is thick, white and has almost tripled in volume, about 12 minutes. Add vanilla and beat 30 seconds to combine. Pour mixture onto prepared jellyroll pans.

Little Helper

Using the spatula, smooth the mixture in the jellyroll pans. Let stand uncovered at room temperature until firm or overnight. When Mommy says the marshmallow mixture is ready, coat a snowflake-shaped cookie cutter with non-stick cooking spray. With Mommy's help, cut out as many marshmallows as possible. Use the marshmallows right away or store in an airtight container.

Puppy Chow

Makes 4 cups

What you'll need

Measuring cups and spoons   Wooden spoon
Large bowl with lid   Waxed paper
Medium saucepan   Bowl

Ingredients

4 C. Chex or Crispix cereal   ¼ C. butter or margarine
½ C. peanut butter   ¼ tsp. vanilla
1 C. chocolate chips   1½ C. powdered sugar

——————————— Little Helper ———————————

With Mommy's help, measure the cereal into the large bowl.

——————————— Mommy ———————————

In the medium saucepan over low heat, place the peanut butter, chocolate chips and butter or margarine. Heat, stirring often,
until completely melted. Remove from heat and stir in vanilla. Pour
melted mixture over cereal in the large bowl.

——————————— Little Helper ———————————

With Mommy's help, stir the cereal mixture until well coated.
Pour in the powdered sugar. Place the lid on the bowl and shake until coated. Remove lid and spread mixture onto the waxed paper.

——————————— Mommy ———————————

Once cooled, place some Puppy Chow in the bowl for your Little Helper. Store remaining Puppy Chow in an airtight container.

Cinnamon &
Sugar Tortilla

Makes 1 serving

What you'll need

Microwave-safe plate

Ingredients

1 flour tortilla　　　　　**Cinnamon**
Butter　　　　　　　　　**Sugar**

―――――――――― **Little Helper** ――――――――――

With Mommy's help, place the tortilla on the microwave-safe plate. Spread the butter all over the tortilla. Sprinkle some cinnamon and sugar all over the tortilla.

―――――――――― **Mommy** ――――――――――

Put the plate in the microwave.

―――――――――― **Little Helper** ――――――――――

With Mommy's help, push the buttons to heat the tortilla for 20 seconds.

―――――――――― **Mommy** ――――――――――

Take plate out of the microwave.

―――――――――― **Little Helper** ――――――――――

When Mommy says the Cinnamon & Sugar Tortilla is ready to eat, roll it up and enjoy!

Cinnamon Twists

Makes 8 servings

What you'll need

Microwave-safe bowl   Baking sheet
Bowl   Plate

Ingredients

½ C. butter   1 C. cinnamon
1 (16 oz.) pkg.   1 T. sugar
   refrigerated biscuits

─── Mommy ───

Place the butter in the microwave-safe bowl and heat in the microwave for 30 seconds, or until completely melted. Mix the cinnamon and sugar in another bowl. Preheat oven to 350°.

─── Little Helper ───

With Mommy's help, stretch the round refrigerated biscuits into an oval shape. Dip into the melted butter, coating both sides. Then dip the biscuits into the cinnamon and sugar mixture, coating both sides. Twist the biscuits about 3 or 4 times in the same direction and place on the baking sheet.

─── Mommy ───

Place the baking sheet into the preheated oven and bake until biscuits are golden brown. When done, remove Cinnamon Twists from oven and place 1 or 2 on the plate for your Little Helper.

Cherry Gelatin Popsicles

Makes 16 servings

What you'll need

Medium bowl   16 popsicle molds
Spoon

Ingredients

1 (6 oz.) pkg. cherry   2 C. boiling water
  flavored gelatin   2 C. fruit juice

--- **Little Helper** ---

With Mommy's help, stir the gelatin into the boiling water, stirring until the gelatin is completely dissolved. Mix in the fruit juice.

--- **Mommy** ---

Pour the liquid into the popsicle molds. Place filled molds into freezer. When the popsicles are frozen, quickly run molds under hot water to release the popsicles and give one to your Little Helper.

Ghostly Nutter Butters

Makes about 24 servings

What you'll need

Double boiler   Plate

Waxed paper

Ingredients

1 (16 oz.) pkg. Nutter   Red hot candies
   Butter cookies   Miniature M&M's
1 (6 oz.) pkg. white   Miniature chocolate chips
   baking chocolate

Mommy

Melt the white baking chocolate in the double boiler over simmering water. Stir often, being careful not to burn the chocolate.

Little Helper

With Mommy's help, dip the Nutter Butter cookies, one at a time, into the melted chocolate. Place the coated cookies on waxed paper to cool.

Mommy

When the white chocolate has hardened, place 1 or 2 cookies on the plate for your Little Helper.

Little Helper

With Mommy's help, decorate the cookies to look like ghosts using the red hot candies, miniature M&M's and miniature chocolate chips. Use additional melted chocolate to attach the decorations to the "ghost" body.

Hamburger Snacker

Makes 1 serving

What you'll need

Plate

Ingredients

1 thin mint   Shredded coconut
2 vanilla wafers

————————————— **Little Helper** —————————————

Unwrap the thin mint "patty" and place it on one of the vanilla wafers. Sprinkle a little shredded coconut over top of the mint patty as the "cheese". Place the other vanilla wafer on top of the coconut. You just made a Hamburger Snacker. Enjoy!

Ice Cream Cone Cupcakes

Makes 16 servings

What you'll need

Large bowl
9 x 13″ baking dish
Toothpick

Wire rack
Butter knife

Ingredients

1 (18 oz.) box yellow
  cake mix

16 ice cream cones
1 (16 oz.) tub frosting

Mommy

Gather the other ingredients needed to prepare for the cake mix according to package directions. Preheat oven according to package directions.

Little Helper

With Mommy's help, prepare the cake mix batter as directed on the box. Fill each ice cream cone ½ full with the batter. Set the cones upright in the baking dish so they won't tip over.

Mommy

Place the baking dish with the filled ice cream cones into the preheated oven. Let your Little Helper test the cupcake cones to see if they are done by inserting a toothpick into the center of a cupcake cone. If the toothpick comes out clean, they're done. Set the baking pan on the wire rack to cool.

Little Helper

With Mommy's help, spread some frosting with the butter knife onto the top of each cupcake cone. Enjoy!

Apple Dip

Makes 4 servings

What you'll need

Medium bowl   Knife

Measuring cups and spoons   Plate

Ingredients

1 (8 oz.) pkg. cream cheese   1 T. vanilla

½ C. brown sugar   Apples

———— Little Helper ————

With Mommy's help, place the cream cheese, brown sugar and vanilla in the medium bowl. Mix until all of the brown sugar has been blended into the cream cheese and vanilla.

———— Mommy ————

With the knife, slice and core the apple. Place the apple slices on the plate for your Little Helper.

———— Little Helper ————

Dip the apple slices in the Apple Dip and enjoy!

Mud Pudding Snacks

Makes 8 servings

What you'll need

Medium bowl

8 disposable cups

Ziplock bag

Rolling pin

Spoon

Ingredients

Instant chocolate pudding

8 gummy worms

8 Oreo cookies

——— Mommy ———

With your Little Helper, prepare chocolate pudding according to package directions. Pour the prepared pudding into the disposable cups, filling each one half full.

——— Little Helper ———

Place 1 gummy worm in each cup on top of the pudding.

——— Mommy ———

Add more pudding to each cup until almost full. Place Oreo cookies into the ziplock bag.

——— Little Helper ———

With Mommy's help, use the rolling pin to crush the cookies in the ziplock bag. Open the bag and sprinkle the crushed cookies over the pudding, filling the cup to the top. Use the spoon to dig in and enjoy one of the Mud Pudding Snacks!

Ladybug Treats

Makes 4 servings

What you'll need

Knife   Small plate

Ingredients

2 red apples   1 T. peanut butter
¼ C. raisins   8 thin pretzel sticks

Mommy

Slice the apples in half from top to bottom. Remove the cores. Place each apple half, flat side down, on the small plate.

Little Helper

With Mommy's help, dab peanut butter on the back of the "ladybug". Stick raisins onto the dabs of peanut butter to make the spots. Stick raisins on the peanut butter to make eyes, too. Stick one end of each pretzel stick into a raisins, then press the other end into the apples to make antennae. Eat your Ladybug Treat and enjoy!

Waffle Sandwich Sundae

Makes 1 serving

What you'll need

Toaster   Plate

Ice cream scoop   Fork

Ingredients

2 frozen waffles   Ice cream toppings

Ice cream

——————————— Little Helper ———————————

With Mommy's help, place the frozen waffles into the toaster and start the toaster.

——————————— Mommy ———————————

When the waffles are done and pop up, place them on the plate.

——————————— Little Helper ———————————

With Mommy's help, scoop some ice cream on top of one waffle. Sprinkle your favorite ice cream toppings over the ice cream. Place the other waffle on top of the ice cream to make a sandwich. Use the fork or pick up with your hands like a sandwich and enjoy!

Snickers Yo-Yo Treats

Makes 15 servings

What you'll need

Butter knife

Microwave-safe bowl

Waxed paper

Plate

Ingredients

1 (9½ oz.) bag M&M's

1 (11 oz.) bag Snickers fun size candy bars

30 (2½") round prepared cookies, any kind

1 tube white decorator's icing

30 (12") pieces red rope licorice

Little Helper

With Mommy's help, use the butter knife to cut up the Snickers candy bars. Place them in the microwave-safe bowl.

Mommy

Place the bowl into the microwave and heat on high for 30 to 40 seconds, until melted and spreadable. Remove bowl from microwave.

Little Helper

With Mommy's help, using the butter knife, spread the softened candy bars on one side of 15 cookies. Place the remaining 15 cookies on top of the softened candy bar to make a sandwich. Place 2 pieces of licorice beside each other and wrap around the candy center, just like a Yo-Yo.

Mommy

When your Little Helper has the licorice around the candy coating, tie a loop for the finger in the end of the licorice.

Little Helper

With Mommy's help, using the decorator's tube of icing, place a dot of icing on the bottom of the M&M's candies. Place one candy in the center of each Yo-Yo. Place the finished Yo-Yo's on waxed paper to let the icing harden. When finished, enjoy one of your Snickers Yo-Yo Treats!

Pudding Pops

Makes 8 servings

What you'll need

Bowl with airtight lid   Popsicle molds
Measuring cup

Ingredients

1 (4 oz.) box instant   3 C. milk
    pudding mix

———————————— **Little Helper** ————————————

With Mommy's help, pour the instant pudding mix into the bowl
and add the milk. Put the lid on the bowl and make sure it's tight.
Shake the bowl with both hands until the pudding is mixed well.

———————————— **Mommy** ————————————

Pour the pudding into the popsicle molds and place in freezer.
When frozen, carefully remove 1 Pudding Pop from the popsicle
mold and give to your Little Helper to enjoy.

Classic Sugar Cookies

Makes 3 to 4 dozen

What you'll need

2 baking sheets
Aluminum foil
Large bowl
Measuring cups and spoons
Kitchen towel

Rolling pin
Cookie cutters
Spatula
Butter knife
Plate

Ingredients

1½ C. powdered sugar
1 C. butter
1 egg
1 tsp. vanilla

3 C. flour
¼ tsp. baking powder
Frosting

Mommy

Preheat oven to 375°. Line the baking sheets with aluminum foil. In the large bowl, cream together the powdered sugar and butter. With your Little Helper, crack the egg into the bowl with the butter mixture. Add the vanilla. Mix well and add the flour and baking powder. Stir until well combined. Cover the bowl with a kitchen towel and place in refrigerator to chill for at least 2 hours. Once chilled, remove from the refrigerator and split the dough in half. Put one half back in the refrigerator.

Little Helper

With Mommy's help, roll half of the dough to ¼″ thickness with the rolling pin on a well floured surface. Use the cookie cutters to cut the dough into shapes. Place the cut out cookie shapes onto the prepared baking sheets.

Mommy

Place the baking sheets in the preheated oven and bake for 8 to 10 minutes. When the cookies are golden brown, remove from oven and transfer to wire racks to cool.

Little Helper

When Mommy says the cookies are cool enough to touch, use the butter knife to frost the cookies and enjoy one or two!

Perfect Cookie Icing

Makes 1 cup

What you'll need

Medium bowl

3 small bowls

Measuring cups and spoons

Ingredients

2 C. powdered sugar

1 tsp. vanilla

3 T. water

Food coloring

--- **Mommy** ---

In the medium bowl, combine the powdered sugar, vanilla and water, mixing until smooth. Separate the frosting into the three small bowls.

--- **Little Helper** ---

With Mommy's help, add one drop of different colored food coloring to each bowl. Add one drop at a time and mix until you have reached the color you want.

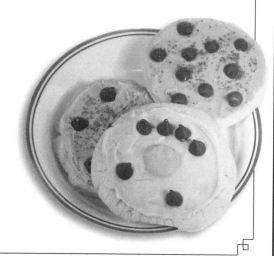

Fudge-a-licious Walnut Brownies

Makes 20 brownies

What you'll need

9 x 13" baking dish
Double boiler
Measuring cups and spoons
Wooden spoon
Medium bowl

Spatula
Toothpick
Butter knife
Plate
Fork

Ingredients

4 (1 oz.) squares unsweetened
    baking chocolate
¾ C. butter
1½ C. sugar
4 eggs

1½ C. flour
2 tsp. baking powder
1 tsp. salt
1 C. chopped walnuts

─────── **Mommy** ───────

Grease the 9 x 13" baking dish. Preheat the oven to 350°. Melt the butter and chocolate in a double boiler over simmering water. When the chocolate and butter are completely melted, remove from heat and add the sugar and eggs. Mix with the wooden spoon until smooth.

─────── **Little Helper** ───────

With Mommy's help, in the medium bowl, combine the flour, baking powder and salt. Add the flour mixture to the chocolate mixture.

─────── **Mommy** ───────

Mix the flour and the chocolate mixture, being careful not to over mix. Stir in the chopped walnuts. Pour the batter into the prepared baking dish.

─────── **Little Helper** ───────

With Mommy's help, smooth the mixture in the pan with the spatula.

─────── **Mommy** ───────

Place the baking dish in the preheated oven and bake for 30 minutes. Remove from oven and let your Little Helper test the doneness by inserting a toothpick into the center of the brownies. If the toothpick comes out clean, the brownies are done. Once the brownies are cooled, remove one brownie and place on the plate for your Little Helper.

No Bake Cookie Crunchies

Makes 2½ dozen

What you'll need

Medium bowl

Measuring cups and spoons

Small saucepan

Wooden spoon

20 mini muffin cup liners

Baking sheet

Plate

Ingredients

4½ C. crushed graham crackers

1 C. chopped peanuts

¼ C. peanut butter

2 C. chocolate chips

1 C. evaporated milk

1 tsp. vanilla

Little Helper

With Mommy's help, combine the crushed graham crackers, chopped peanuts and peanut butter in the medium bowl.

Mommy

In the small saucepan over low heat, combine the chocolate chips and evaporated milk, stirring constantly until melted and smooth. Remove from the heat and stir in the vanilla. Pour the chocolate mixture over the crumb mixture in the bowl.

Little Helper

With Mommy's help, stir the chocolate mixture and crumb mixture together until well blended. Set mini muffin cups on a baking sheet.

Mommy

Fill each mini muffin cup ¾ full with the peanut-cookie mixture. Place in refrigerator for 1 hour until they are firm. Remove from refrigerator and place 1 or 2 on a plate for your Little Helper.

Mini Ice Cream Sandwiches

Makes 1 dozen

What you'll need

Ice cream scoop   Baking sheet
Butter knife   Plate

Ingredients

24 chocolate cookie wafers   Chocolate sauce
1 pint ice cream, softened

――――――――――――― **Little Helper** ―――――――――――――

With Mommy's help, lay the chocolate wafers, flat side up, on
the counter or on the table. Place a small scoop of ice cream on 12
of the wafers. Top with the remaining 12 wafers. Firmly push them
together, but not so much that the ice cream squishes out the sides.
If this happens, take a butter knife and smooth out the sides. Place
the sandwiches on the baking sheet.

――――――――――――― **Mommy** ―――――――――――――

Place the baking sheet in the freezer for 2 hours. When firm, remove from freezer. Place 1 or 2 on the plate for your Little Helper.

――――――――――――― **Little Helper** ―――――――――――――

With Mommy's help, place some chocolate sauce in a small bowl.
Dip your ice cream sandwich in the chocolate sauce and enjoy!

Cream Biscuits

Makes 8 to 10 servings

What you'll need

Baking sheet

Aluminum foil

Measuring cups and spoons

Medium bowl

Rolling pin

Biscuit cutter

Pastry brush

Plate

Ingredients

2½ C. flour

½ tsp. salt

1 T. baking powder

2 T. sugar

1⅓ C. plus 2 T. heavy whipping cream, divided

——————— Mommy ———————

Preheat oven to 400°. Line the baking sheet with aluminum foil.

——————— Little Helper ———————

With Mommy's help, combine the flour, salt, baking powder and sugar in the medium bowl. Stir in 1⅓ cups of the heavy cream and mix lightly until a dough begins to form.

——————— Mommy ———————

Use the rolling pin to roll the dough out on a well floured surface to ½″ thickness.

——————— Little Helper ———————

With Mommy's help, cut the rolled dough with the biscuit cutter. Place the biscuits on the prepared baking sheet. With the pastry brush, brush the tops with the remaining 2 tablespoons heavy cream.

——————— Mommy ———————

Place the baking sheet in the preheated oven and bake for 12 to 15 minutes. When the tops are golden brown, remove from oven and place one on the plate for your Little Helper.

Strawberry Shortcakes

Makes 6 servings

What you'll need

Measuring cups and spoons
Medium bowl
Butter knife

6 plates
6 forks

Ingredients

6 Cream Biscuits
  (recipe on page 95)
3 C. sliced strawberries

Juice of ½ lemon
1 T. honey
Whipped topping

Mommy

Prepare the Cream Biscuits according to the recipe on page 95.

Little Helper

With Mommy's help, combine the sliced strawberries, lemon juice and honey in the medium bowl. With the butter knife, slice the Cream Biscuits in half and place each one on a plate. Place a scoop of the strawberries on the bottom half and follow with a spoonful of whipped topping. Place the top half on the shortcake. Spoon on a few more strawberries over top and add a dollop of whipped topping on each. Serve with the forks and enjoy!

Vanilla
Whipped Cream

Makes 4 cups

What you'll need

Medium bowl   Whisk

Ingredients

2 C. heavy whipping cream   1 tsp. vanilla
2 T. powdered sugar

──────────────── Little Helper ────────────────

With Mommy's help, combine the whipping cream, powdered
sugar and vanilla in the medium bowl. Beat with a whisk until firm
peaks form.

──────────────── Mommy ────────────────

If your Little Helper gets tired, you can finish the beating with the
whisk. Be careful not to over mix. Serve over hot drinks or with cake
or brownies or in recipes calling for whipped cream or topping.

Chocolate Chip Cheese Ball

Makes about 32 servings

What you'll need

Medium bowl

Measuring cups and spoons

Plastic wrap

Plate

Ingredients

1 (8 oz.) pkg. cream cheese, softened

½ C. butter, softened

¾ C. powdered sugar

2 T. brown sugar

¼ tsp. vanilla

¾ C. miniature chocolate chips

¾ C. finely chopped pecans

——————— **Little Helper** ———————

With Mommy's help, place the cream cheese and softened butter into the medium bowl and beat together. Mix in the powdered sugar, brown sugar and vanilla. Stir in the chocolate chips.

——————— **Mommy** ———————

Cover the cream cheese mixture in the bowl with plastic wrap. Place in the refrigerator to chill. Remove from refrigerator after 2 hours.

——————— **Little Helper** ———————

With Mommy's help, shape the cream cheese mixture into a ball.

——————— **Mommy** ———————

Wrap the ball with plastic wrap. Place in the refrigerator to chill. Remove the ball after 1 hour. Remove the plastic wrap from the ball.

——————— **Little Helper** ———————

With Mommy's help, roll the cheese ball in finely chopped pecans. Place the ball on the plate and serve with graham crackers, small cookies and fruit for dipping.

Snacks
&
Mixes

Cracker Pizzas

Makes 4 servings

What you'll need

Shallow baking pan
Non-stick spray
Butter knife

Spoon
Plate

Ingredients

12 wheat crackers
1½ oz. slice mozzarella cheese

¼ C. pizza sauce
Sliced, pitted ripe olives

Mommy

Preheat the oven broiler.

Little Helper

With Mommy's help, arrange the wheat crackers in the shallow baking pan that has been lightly greased with non-stick cooking spray. With the butter knife, cut the cheese slice in half lengthwise, then into sixths crosswise, making 12 squares. Place a piece of cheese on each cracker. Spoon about 1 teaspoon pizza sauce on top over each cracker and top with a few olive slices.

Mommy

Place the baking sheet under the preheated broiler 5″ to 6″ below the heat for 1 to 2 minutes. When cheese is melted, remove from broiler. Place 1 or 2 on the plate for your Little Helper.

Super-Duper Strawberry Bars

Makes 12 servings

What you'll need

Large bowl	Large spoon
Measuring cups and spoons	Butter knife
8″ square baking dish	Plate
Non-stick cooking spray	

Ingredients

1 C. flour	¼ tsp. baking powder
1 C. rolled oats	⅛ tsp. salt
½ C. butter, softened	¾ C. strawberry jam
⅓ C. brown sugar	

Mommy

Preheat oven to 350°. Coat the 8″ square baking dish with the non-stick cooking spray.

Little Helper

With Mommy's help, combine the flour, rolled oats, butter, brown sugar, baking powder and salt in the large bowl.

Mommy

Measure out 2 cups of this mixture and set aside the remainder in the bowl for later.

Little Helper

With Mommy's help, press the 2 cups of the mixture into the bottom of the prepared baking dish. Using a large spoon, spread the strawberry jam evenly over top of the mixture in the pan. Take the mixture that was left in the large bowl and spread it over the strawberry jam. Press down lightly with the back of the spoon.

Mommy

Place the baking dish in the preheated oven and bake for 25 minutes. Remove from the oven and let cool for at least 15 minutes. Cut into 12 squares. Place 1 serving on the plate for your Little Helper.

Ants On A Log

Makes 1 serving

What you'll need

Butter knife   Plate

Ingredients

Celery stalks   Raisins
Peanut butter

———————————— **Mommy** ————————————
Thoroughly wash the celery stalks, removing any leaves.

———————————— **Little Helper** ————————————
With Mommy's help, using the butter knife, cut the celery into 4″ lengths. Spread the peanut butter on the celery pieces. Add several raisins on top of the peanut butter and enjoy!

PB & J Waffle Bites

Makes 2 servings

What you'll need

Toaster   Butter knife
Plate

Ingredients

4 miniature frozen waffles   1 T. peanut butter
1 banana   1 T. jelly

Mommy

Place the frozen waffles in the toaster and toast until golden brown. Place the toasted waffles on the plate and separate into individual pieces. Cut the banana into thin slices.

Little Helper

With Mommy's help, using butter knife, spread peanut butter on 2 of the miniature waffles. Spread jelly on top of the peanut butter. Place the banana slice on top of the jelly. Then place the remaining miniature waffles on top. Enjoy!

Basic Applesauce

Makes about 4 quarts

What you'll need

Knife   Measuring cups and spoons
Large pot   Canning jars
Strainer   Canner

Ingredients

30 to 35 fresh apples   Brown sugar
¾ C. water   1 tsp. cinnamon

———————————— **Mommy** ————————————

Peel and core the apples. Cut the cored apples into quarters

———————————— **Little Helper** ————————————

With Mommy's help, place the apples in the large pot. Add the water and cook over medium heat until the apples are soft, stirring frequently.

———————————— **Mommy** ————————————

Push the cooked apples through a strainer or use an applesauce grinder. While warm, add the brown sugar to taste. Stir in the cinnamon. Pour the applesauce into pint or quart size canning jars. Process in a boiling water bath canner at 20 minutes for pints and 25 minutes for quart jars.

Chocolate Chip Banana Bread

Makes 1 loaf

What you'll need

5 x 9″ loaf pan
Non-stick cooking spray
Large mixing bowl
Measuring cups and spoons

Electric mixer
Wooden toothpick
Wire rack

Ingredients

2 C. flour
1 C. sugar
1 tsp. baking powder
1 tsp. salt
½ tsp. baking soda

1 C. mashed ripe banana
½ C. vegetable oil
2 eggs
1 C. miniature chocolate chips
½ C. finely chopped pecans

Mommy

Spray the 5 x 9″ loaf pan with non-stick cooking spray and set aside. Preheat oven to 350°.

Little Helper

With Mommy's help, combine the flour, sugar, baking powder, salt, baking soda, mashed banana, vegetable oil and eggs in the large bowl.

Mommy

Beat with the mixer at medium speed until well blended.

Little Helper

With Mommy's help, stir in the miniature chocolate chips and chopped pecans. Pour the batter into the prepared pan.

Mommy

Place the filled loaf pan in the preheated oven and bake for 60 to 65 minutes or until a wooden toothpick inserted in the center comes out clean. Remove from oven and cool for 10 minutes before removing from the pan to a wire rack. Cut a slice for your Little Helper.

Rainbow Trail Mix

Makes about 4 cups

What you'll need

Large bowl

Measuring cups

Airtight container

Small ziplock bags

Ingredients

1 (14 oz.) bag M&M's candies

2 C. popped popcorn

½ C. dry roasted peanuts

½ C. banana chips

½ C. dried cranberries

½ C. raisins

───────────── **Little Helper** ─────────────

With Mommy's help, combine the M&M's, popped popcorn, peanuts, banana chips, dried cranberries and raisins in the large bowl. Gently toss all the ingredients. Pour the mix into an airtight container.

───────────── **Mommy** ─────────────

Scoop some of the Rainbow Trail Mix into a small ziplock bag for your Little Helper.

Fresh Homemade Chips

Makes 8 to 10 servings

What you'll need

Butter knife
Metal tong
Deep iron skillet

Plate
Paper towel
Small bowl

Ingredients

½ pkg. two day old tortillas
Vegetable oil

2 tsp. cinnamon
⅓ C. sugar

─────────── **Mommy** ───────────

Cut the slightly stale tortillas into wedges and separate. Place about 1″ vegetable oil in the deep skillet. Heat oil over medium high heat.

─────────── **Little Helper** ───────────

With Mommy's help, take the metal tong and pick up one piece of the tortilla at a time. Gently place each tortilla in the hot oil. Turn the chips over when they turn light tan. Tell Mommy to remove each chip with the metal tong when both sides are tan in color. Place the chips on paper towels to drain.

─────────── **Mommy** ───────────

In the small bowl, combine the cinnamon and sugar. Have your Little Helper sprinkle the sugar mixture over the chips.

The "Elvis"

Makes 1 serving

What you'll need

Butter knife   Plate

Ingredients

1 banana   Marshmallow cream
Peanut butter   2 slices wheat bread

————————— **Mommy** —————————

Cut the banana into slices with the butter knife and set aside.

————————— **Little Helper** —————————

Place 1 slice wheat bread on the plate. Using the butter knife, spread peanut butter over one slice of bread. Spread the marshmallow cream over the other slice of bread. Place the banana slices over the peanut butter. Place the other slice of bread with the marshmallow creme over top. Enjoy!

Crunchy Munch

Makes 20 servings

What you'll need

Microwave
Measuring cups and spoons
Large brown paper bag

Microwave-safe bowl
Small bowl

Ingredients

3 (3½ oz.) bags microwave
  popcorn
1 (12 oz.) jar dry roasted
  peanuts
1 C. brown sugar

½ C. margarine
¼ C. corn syrup
½ tsp. salt
½ tsp. baking soda

—————————— Mommy ——————————

Pop the 3 bags of microwave popcorn in microwave according to package directions.

—————————— Little Helper ——————————

Put the popped popcorn and peanuts into the large brown paper bag.

—————————— Mommy ——————————

Combine the brown sugar, margarine, corn syrup, salt and baking soda in a microwave-safe bowl. Place in microwave and cook on high for 2 minutes. Remove from microwave and pour into the large brown paper bag. Close the bag tightly and give to your Little Helper.

—————————— Little Helper ——————————

Shake the bag thoroughly, until Mommy says it's ready. Give the paper bag to Mommy.

—————————— Mommy ——————————

Pour some of the Crunchy Munch into the small bowl for your Little Helper.

Screaming Deviled Eggs

Makes 12 servings

What you'll need

Butter knife

Measuring spoons

Small bowl

Fork

Covered container

Ingredients

6 hard-boiled eggs

3 T. mayonnaise

1 tsp. Dijon mustard

12 olive slices

24 capers

Mommy

Slice each hard-boiled egg in half with the butter knife and gently remove the yolk, being careful not to break the white.

Little Helper

With Mommy's help, place the yolks in the small bowl and mash with the back of the fork. Add the mayonnaise and mustard and mix until smooth.

Mommy

With a teaspoon, fill the hollowed egg whites with the yolk mixture and smooth the tops with the back of a dinner knife. Place the deviled eggs in the container.

Little Helper

With Mommy's help, decorate each egg with an olive slice for the mouth and capers for the eyes.

Mommy

Cover the container and place in the refrigerator until ready to serve.

Quick Croutons

Makes 54 croutons

What you'll need

Butter knife   Small saucepan
Large bowl   Baking sheet
Measuring cups and spoons

Ingredients

6 slices whole wheat bread   ¼ C. Parmesan cheese
3 T. butter   Salt and pepper

Mommy

Preheat oven to 275°.

Little Helper

With Mommy's help, cut each slice of bread into 9 cubes using the butter knife. Place the bread cubes in the large bowl.

Mommy

Melt the butter over low heat in the small saucepan. Pour the melted butter over bread cubes in the bowl.

Little Helper

With Mommy's help, add the Parmesan cheese to the bread cubes. Toss until well mixed and all the butter has been absorbed. Spread the croutons on the baking sheet.

Mommy

Sprinkle the bread pieces lightly with salt and pepper. Place the croutons in the preheated oven and bake for 30 minutes or until each crouton is slightly browned and very crisp. Remove from the oven and let cool.

Fruit Kabobs

What you'll need

Melon baller   Plate

Skewers

Ingredients

Strawberries   Orange sections

Grapes   Banana pieces

Cantaloupe   Fruit flavored yogurt

Honeydew melon

────────────── **Mommy** ──────────────

Use a melon baller to scoop balls from the cantaloupe and honeydew melon.

────────────── **Little Helper** ──────────────

With Mommy's help, take the fruit pieces and slide them onto the skewer in any order you want. Place the finished skewers on the plate.

────────────── **Mommy** ──────────────

Place the plate with the finished skewers in the refrigerator. When ready to serve, remove from the refrigerator. Place the fruit yogurt in a bowl for dipping and give one Fruit Kabob to your Little Helper.

On-The-Go Squares

Makes 12 servings

What you'll need

Large bowl

Measuring cups

Non-stick spray

10″ square baking dish

Plate

Ingredients

3 C. granola

1 C. old fashioned oats

¼ C. honey

1 egg, beaten

½ C. peanut butter

———————— **Mommy** ————————

Preheat oven to 350°. Grease 10″ square baking dish with the non-stick spray.

———————— **Little Helper** ————————

With Mommy's help, combine the granola, old fashioned oats, honey, egg and peanut butter in the large bowl. Mix thoroughly. Press mixture into the prepared baking dish.

———————— **Mommy** ————————

Place the baking dish in the preheated oven and bake for 20 minutes. Remove from oven when done. When cool, cut into 12 squares. Place one square on the plate for your Little Helper.

Animal Food

Makes 4 servings

What you'll need

Large bowl
Measuring cups

Small ziplock bags

Ingredients

2 C. animal shaped
   graham crackers
1 C. salted peanuts

½ C. M&M's candies
½ C. raisins

—————————— **Little Helper** ——————————

With Mommy's help, combine the animal crackers, salted peanuts, M&M's candies and raisins in the large bowl. Mix together.

—————————— **Mommy** ——————————

Divide the mixture into small ziplock bags and give one to your Little Helper to enjoy.

Awesome Cinnamon Applesauce

Makes 2 servings

What you'll need

Knife   2 small bowls
Blender   2 spoons
Measuring spoons

Ingredients

2 red apples   2 tsp. sugar
2 T. lemon juice   2 pinches cinnamon

––––––––––––––––– **Mommy** –––––––––––––––––

Peel the apples and cut them into small pieces.

––––––––––––––––– **Little Helper** –––––––––––––––––

With Mommy's help, place the apple pieces and lemon juice in the blender.

––––––––––––––––– **Mommy** –––––––––––––––––

Place the lid on the blender. Show your Little Helper the button to push to liquefy the mixture. Once blended, pour the mixture into 2 small bowls. Stir half of the sugar and cinnamon into the applesauce in each bowl. Give one bowl to your Little Helper.

––––––––––––––––– **Little Helper** –––––––––––––––––

Pick up your spoon and enjoy your Awesome Cinnamon Applesauce!

Homemade Granola

Makes about 6 cups

What you'll need

Measuring cups and spoons   Medium bowl
Large bowl   Baking sheet

Ingredients

3 C. rolled oats   ½ C. golden raisins
½ C. whole wheat flour   Pinch of salt
1 C. shredded coconut   ½ C. honey
½ C. sunflower seeds   ¼ C. vegetable oil
½ C. chopped nuts   ¼ C. hot water
½ C. chopped, dried apricots   1 tsp. vanilla

Mommy

Preheat oven to 250°.

Little Helper

With Mommy's help, combine the rolled oats, whole wheat flour, shredded coconut, sunflower seeds, chopped nuts, chopped apricots, golden raisins and salt in the large bowl.

Mommy

In the medium bowl, combine the honey, vegetable oil, hot water and vanilla and mix thoroughly. Pour the wet ingredients over the dry mixture and stir until well combined.

Little Helper

With Mommy's help, spread the mixture evenly on the baking sheet.

Mommy

Place the baking sheet in the preheated oven and bake for 1 hour and 15 minutes. When done, remove from oven and let cool.

Frozen Applesauce & Fruit Cup

Makes 7 servings

What you'll need

Measuring cups and spoons
Medium bowl

Paper cups
Spoon

Ingredients

1 C. chunky applesauce
1 (10 oz.) pkg. frozen, sliced
  strawberries, thawed
1 (11 oz.) can mandarin
  orange segments, drained

1 C. grapes
2 C. orange juice concentrate

——————————— Little Helper ———————————

With Mommy's help, combine the applesauce, sliced strawberries, mandarin orange segments, grapes and orange juice concentrate in the medium bowl. Mix well and divide the fruit mixture into the individual paper cups.

——————————— Mommy ———————————

Place the paper cups in the freezer and freeze until firm. Remove from the freezer and let thaw at room temperature for about 30 minutes before serving. Give one to your Little Helper.

——————————— Little Helper ———————————

Dig into the Frozen Applesauce & Fruit Cup with the spoon. Enjoy!

Munching Goldfish & Friends

Makes about 4 cups

What you'll need

11 x 17″ jellyroll pan   Measuring cups and spoons
Non-stick cooking spray   2 small bowls
Large bowl   Airtight container

Ingredients

¾ C. Corn Chex   ¾ C. pretzel nuggets
1½ C. goldfish crackers   1½ T. soy sauce
¾ C. Cheerios   2 tsp. Dijon mustard
½ C. graham cracker   1 tsp. garlic powder
   Teddy Bears   1 tsp. onion powder

Mommy

Grease the jellyroll pan with the non-stick cooking spray. Preheat oven to 350°.

Little Helper

With Mommy's help, combine the Corn Chex, goldfish crackers, Cheerios, graham cracker Teddy Bears and pretzel nuggets in the large bowl. In one of the small bowls, combine the soy sauce, Dijon mustard, garlic powder and onion powder, mixing until blended well.

Mommy

Pour the sauce mixture over the cereal mixture and toss until well combined. Spread mixture into the prepared pan. Place pan in preheated oven and bake for 5 minutes. Remove mixture from oven and mix lightly. Return the pan to the oven and bake for an additional 5 minutes. Remove from oven and cool completely. Place some of the Munching Goldfish & Friends in the remaining small bowl and give to your Little Helper to enjoy. Store the remaining mixture in an airtight container.

Amazing Apple Crunch

Makes 8 servings

What you'll need

9 x 13″ baking dish
Non-stick cooking spray
Small bowl

Measuring cups and spoons
Plate
Fork

Ingredients

8 apples
⅓ C. orange juice
1 C. brown sugar
1 C. rolled oats

½ C. butter, softened
2 tsp. cinnamon
¼ C. flour

Mommy

Grease the 9 x 13″ baking dish with the non-stick cooking spray. Preheat oven to 375°. Slice the apples into thin wedges.

Little Helper

With Mommy's help, spread the apples evenly in the prepared baking pan. Pour the orange juice over the apples. In the small bowl, combine the brown sugar, rolled oats, butter, cinnamon and flour. With your clean hands, crumble this mixture on top of the apples and orange juice mixture.

Mommy

Place the baking pan in the preheated oven and bake for 40 minutes. Remove from oven and let cool. Once cooled, cut into squares. Place one serving on the plate for your Little Helper.

Fun Pretzels

Makes 25 pretzels

What you'll need

Medium bowl	Small bowl
Measuring cups and spoons	Pastry brush
2 baking sheets	Plate
Non-stick cooking spray	

Ingredients

2 (1 oz.) pkgs. dry yeast	4 C. flour
1½ C. warm water	1 egg
1 tsp. salt	Coarse salt
1 tsp. sugar	

—————————— **Mommy** ——————————

Preheat oven to 425°. Grease the baking sheets with the non-stick cooking spray.

—————————— **Little Helper** ——————————

With Mommy's help, dissolve the yeast in warm water in the medium bowl. Add salt and sugar. Blend in the flour.

—————————— **Mommy** ——————————

On a lightly floured flat surface, knead the dough until smooth. Cut the dough into 25 small pieces.

—————————— **Little Helper** ——————————

With Mommy's help, roll the small pieces into ropes. Twist each rope into pretzel shapes or make your own shapes. Place the finished shapes on the prepared baking sheets.

—————————— **Mommy** ——————————

Crack the egg into the small bowl and beat well.

—————————— **Little Helper** ——————————

With Mommy's help, use the pastry brush to brush the beaten egg over the pretzel shapes. Sprinkle coarse salt over the pretzels.

—————————— **Mommy** ——————————

Place the baking sheets in the preheated oven for 12 to 15 minutes. Once pretzels are golden brown, remove from oven and let cool slightly. Place one or two on the plate for your Little Helper.

Index

Treats, Cookies & Desserts